About the author

My name is Sheila and I am the daughter of circus and fair ground people. I did not learn to read and write until I was thirty-one years of age. I have four children, fourteen grandchildren and twelve great-grandchildren, and now that I am seventy-eight, I am finally getting my book published. I started to write my book in 1983, some twenty-seven years ago. My book has been read by many people. I have even read it to school children and my church club. I also write poetry as a hobby for the church magazine.

THE HOP PICKERS' CHILDREN

SHEILA JUDITH ANNE AYRES

THE HOP PICKERS' CHILDREN

Vanguard Press

A CIP catalogue record for this title is
available from the British Library.

ISBN 978 1 784659 02 8

*Vanguard Press is an imprint of
Pegasus Elliot MacKenzie Publishers Ltd.*
www.pegasuspublishers.com

First Published in 2021

**Vanguard Press
Sheraton House Castle Park
Cambridge England**

Printed & Bound in Great Britain

Dedication

I dedicate this book to my father, Charles Ayres, to thank him for teaching me the true value of life, and also my mother, Jemima.

"Possessions can be taken from you at any time, but the gifts of nature are all around for each and every one of us if we only stop to look at them".

Also, to my dear husband who drew all the pictures, may he rest in peace.

Dear children and grandchildren,

I am writing this book for you so that you can read it when I am no longer with you. Although you don't walk and talk Carly dear, I hope someone will read it to you. I hope you all get great pleasure from reading it, as it gave me such pleasure to write it all down for you.

If....... as I hope, you enjoy the simple things in life such as the gifts of nature, and then I know you will enjoy reading it. However, if it is the worldly things you expect to get in life like wealth and being famous, this book is not for you.

We bring nothing into this world and we take nothing out, but I hope to leave you all a lasting treasure of my memories in this my story. Although the people in it are long gone, I hope that you are able to picture them in your mind's eye and enjoy what my mind and heart want to tell you.

This story was lived a long ago when I was a small child. This is my story of the hop picker children and their family's descendants. It's about how we lived and specifically how I was brought up. A bloody poor man's holiday, was what my mother called it, so that is what I shall call it myself.

Contents

THE STORY BEGINS

This is the story of the children of Jemima and Charlie growing up in the years just after the war in 1945. This is the beginning of my era, second born to Charlie and Jemima.

We came from a mixed background of fair and circus people to log and flower sellers, and although we no longer roamed the roads, we still trekked off each year to go on our hop picking holiday.

This is a true account of what went on as far as I can remember it. Hop picking was a poor man's holiday and the only one we could afford. It was more of a break than anything else. It meant we could go away each year to see old friends and relations. Our education suffered quite a bit as a result. My being dyslexic didn't help matters. It made no difference to our parents that we were unable to read. They went year after year until the arrival of the hop picking machines.

This is my story of the Ayres family and their relations, written by me, Sheila Ayres, the daughter of Charles and Jemima Ayres. I put off writing this book because of my dyslexia and lack of confidence, but I feel I must leave a record of how we all lived. Although this is not written down in the correct manner, I hope I can give you an insight into our lives when we went away each year. I have written it as close to the facts as I can recall them.

All the illustrations are by my husband and artist, Norman John Standing.

PREFACE

Hello, my name is Sheila Ayres, and I am writing this book as my historical biography.

The events in this book are true facts that were handed down over the years to me and my family, and it all started many years ago when a prince took a liking to one of my ancestors.

It was a dark winter's evening. The fairground gypsies all sang and danced round the fire, and as they were in their resting quarters at Windsor, they were not far from the palace walls. Many a night the prince would come down to watch the gypsies. He was fascinated by them and enjoyed the entertainment of watching them dance. Well, of watching one particular individual dance. The story was foretold by a member of my family, who was told by pain of death to not repeat it. Hence the dates and names of the first part of my history cannot be told in respect of that.

The prince would come down to watch the party of the gypsies every night until, one night, he took one of the gypsy girls aside. It was said he had a great affection for her beauty, and he told her of his affection. Just like all young girls, she was wooed by the prince and fell in love with him. The prince and the gypsy girl knew that it could not last as they were never to marry. Unfortunately, the gypsy girl gave herself to the prince and became pregnant. Certain dignitaries were involved and a small amount of land was given as compensation. The gypsies were asked to move on and by pain of death to not repeat to another soul how the child to be born, was of royal descent.

Hence my history was born. This book is a story of how the generations became what they are today, general families living in general housing. It is a story of a bygone era and an insight into the Jones/Cooper dynasty. It will make you laugh and make you cry. It will give you a background into what it was like at the fair living as fairground people and then what it was like to travel and pick hops and how beer was made. This is not just a fairy tale life but a true life that was lived by my ancestors. We think that they had it hard but, on reflection, I feel they had the best of this world.

My daughter, Penny, has helped me to finish this book and to her I give the credit of the time she has spent retyping and helping me. I myself did not learn to read or write until I was in my thirties. I sometimes struggle with the concept of grammar and have told this book in my own words. The story of the prince at Windsor was passed onto my first-born, Penny, by my Uncle Sammy on a summer's day in 1984 and she has not forgotten a word told to her since. She feels it is time to pass on the story as many centuries have passed.

THE LETTER

It was in the year 1945 in the month of August that I first recall going hop picking. My brother, Charlie, and I were with our mother in our little two-room bungalow at Field Common, on the outskirts of the little village called Hersham. My mother was making pastry at the time the post arrived. Dropping bits of pastry, we ran to the door to get the letters, crashing into furniture as we went. Charlie laughed as he snatched the letters from Pop Smith's hand. Pop brought us our letters on a Sunday and he sold sweets as well. He had the post office shop in Hersham village.

"Got 'em," Charlie yelled. I fought to control the tears that filled my eyes. "You big baby, I ain't touched ya and ya crying like a baby," he said. "Just because I got the letter first you ave ta cry."

Mum took the letters from him. "Oh, no," she said. "I know what this is for before I open it." Sitting down, she opened the letter, shaking her head from side to side as she did so.

"What's it say, Mum?" I asked "What's it for?"

"What's it for," she said in a sad voice. "Hopping, bloody hop picking; it's our so-called holiday. It's a bloody poor man's holiday."

I gazed at her sad face, not understanding all the fuss. I had no memory of going the previous year as I was just four years old. Charlie was eighteen months older than me so he knew all about it. Charlie began to jump up and down with excitement singing, "We're going hopping!" as he did so.

That afternoon when my father came home from work Charlie ran to greet him. "Dad, Dad," he yelled "the letter's come, it's come."

Dad's face beamed. "What letter?" he asked.

"This letter, as well you know, Charlie Ayres," Mum snapped. "The letter you ave been expecting all week," she said, throwing it across the table towards him.

Dad just laughed at her. "You know you like it, Mima," he said, "so don't keep on so."

"Like it, like it," she screamed. "It's not what I call a holiday, that's for sure. It's just hard work for me. All I do is slog me guts out, but that makes no odds to you. You don't care so long as you can go with the rest of your family. That's all that matters to you."

THE DEPARTURE

It was a week later that we went. I can still picture it. Mrs Wright, the little woman in the bungalow next to ours, was standing with her fat arms around Mum. She brushed a stray curl away from Mum's face. "There, there, my ducks, it's not forever," she said. "Just a few weeks that's all."

Mum cried, "But I don't want to go to that place with my kids, they'll freeze to death in them tin huts. They had bad coughs the last time we came back from that god forsaken place. It's all right fer im, ee don't ave ta slog like me, Oh no."

"I tell you what," said Mrs Wright, "you drop me a line before you get back, my ducks and I'll get a fire going and air the place out for you." She gave her a hug and continued to reassure her. Finally, the little cart was loaded, and we were on our way, but not until Mrs Wright had given Mum a final hug, as she was just like a mother to our mum.

I remember sitting on the back of the cart with Charlie in a harness made of Dad's old ties and string. He made them to prevent us from falling off. Our legs dangled over the tail board at the back, and our old mongrel dog sat in between. The scruffiest dog you have ever seen. Charlie was singing at the top of his voice, "We're going hopping," as we waved to Mrs Wright until she was out of sight. Down the bumpy lane we went. We were the hop pickers' children and we were so happy.

THE JOURNEY

We were to meet my father's brothers and sisters in one of the many pubs that lined our route, as we had to make frequent stops to give the horse water and let him rest. The pub I liked best was called the Cricketers. It was a small pub and it overlooked a large green. There was a pond with willows growing at one side of it. Ducks swam on the water; Charlie threw bread to them. It was a sunny day and we loved it. Mum was feeding our horse from a nose bag whilst Dad was in the pub with his family, drinking. He sent us out a drink of ginger beer in a stone bottle, and one for Mum as she did not drink alcohol like his family. Then we sat on the grass dozing in the sun until my father came out and we continued our journey.

If I close my eyes, I can still picture the narrow winding roads, with hedgerows overgrown, as our tired old horse plodded on. We had travelled for what seemed like hours to me and indeed it had been.

BINSTEAD

"Look, Charlie, look, Shill," said Dad at last. "It's Binstead."

"Good job too," said Mum. "I thought we would never get here; it'll be dark soon."

"Oh, leave off, Mima, don't start," Dad replied.

Charlie and me scrambled to the top of the cart, straining to see. In the middle of the road was a signpost sticking out of a mound of earth. We were at the crossroads to the little village of Binstead, near Alton in Hampshire. Directly in front was a village school built high on a hill. There was a flight of steps leading up to it, a hand rail to the right of them. To the right of that there was a large tree, its exposed roots dangling from the bank like a giant octopus. Directly at the side of the school a narrow road wound its way upwards, towards the church and the King's Arms pub.

The road to the left was the one we wanted, past the kiln and up a narrow winding road with its hedgerows overgrown. There were a few houses dotted along the top at the right-hand side. Our old horse strained as it made its way along the road.

Soon it widened. Dad stopped. He sat staring at the two pubs that faced each other. "Ain't that a pretty sight," he said, as he removed his trilby hat and fanned his flushed face with it. Giving a deep sigh he ran his fingers through his dark lank hair.

Oh, the White Hart, what a sight, all whitewashed with a thatched roof and a small sloping lawn in the front. To its right was a stone wall all covered in green and grey moss. The Cedars, on the other side, was a plain pub in comparison. It had a red brick wall built in front of it, with rings set in it for the horses to be tied to, as a lot of people still used horses as a means of transport. In the middle of the wall was a flight of steps that forked left and right at the top, and at the right of the wall at its side was another flight that went to a little shop, that belonged to the pub. The publican's wife managed the shop. At the top of the left flight of steps in the middle of the wall was a patch of rough grass. This had railings along two sides of it, around three feet off the ground, the sort that you could swing over on your stomach. We were often to do this in the years to come.

"Come on, Charlie Ayres," Mum moaned. "ain't you had enough drink for one day? surely you don't want more, man."

"Oh, leave off, woman," Dad said as he urged the horse onward to Hay Place Farm.

Soon we came to a big gate. "Whoa," said Dad pulling back on the reins. "This is it." Looking up, I saw a large white stone barn with a grey slate roof to it. At one end there was straw and hay and at the other a stable. At the side of that was a lean-to made of corrugated tin. It had a big cart in it. "Open the gate, Charlie," said Dad. "Make sure ya shut it after ya, tho."

A man came out of the lean-to. He was the carter, Dad said. Touching his cap, he said, "Evening, Charlie, evening, missus. See you're back agin, then." Dad smiled. Mum sat as though she were made of stone. The carter put a knurled hand on Charlie's head as he shut the gate behind us. In front of us was a large field with trees all around it. Charlie climbed back onto the cart and Dad urged our horse onward over the bumpy ground, past the bow-bender tents that the hedge-mumpers lived in, as that's what my father called the people that lived in them. The reason their tents were called bow-benders was because they were made from the bent boughs of small trees that grew at the side of the field, preferably over a ditch. They threw tarpaulins over them to keep out the weather, and they were a really rough lot, I can tell you. Dad said we were never to go near them, as they were not to be trusted and he feared for our safety.

Directly to our left was a ramshackle brick building and a few tin huts. Further over at the back of the field stood a black chicken hut with wire mesh at its windows, a short distance from that a row of tin huts. The huts were made of tin with corrugated tin roofs and they were about eight feet square. They had no windows and no locks on the doors. There was just a piece of wire to make a latch. Dotted around the field was an occasional tent and caravan.

Mum gave a deep sigh as the cart came to a final halt. "Don't run off," she said. "I need some help." The place was a hive of activity, with people unloading their few meagre possessions, such as they were. I could see my aunts and uncles with their children. The older boys were fighting over who it was that would get to sleep in the shepherd's hut on wheels that stood out in the field.

GETTING THE WATER

Charlie walked about talking to this one and that, but I didn't know them. They knew him well enough, though. "Coming with us, Charlie?" they asked.

"No," he replied, "I gotta git me mum some water first."

Mum's voice cut across the conversation. "I thought I told you to get the water," she said sternly, "not stand there gassing."

"Can I come, Charlie?" I asked him.. "Let me come."

"No, you ain't," he yelled. "Ya can't come."

Dad shouted at him, "You take your sister with you, old man, or your feel the back of my hand. Take her to the tap for water like I told ya to."

Charlie picked up a large black kettle, swinging it as he went. I ran after him trying to catch up. "Come on then," he yelled." I can't hang on all day, yer know."

The tap was by the stables at the horse trough. It was just in front of it in fact. By the time we reached it, there was a long queue of children all shoving each other to get at it.

I don't think that I have ever seen so much mud as there was at the tap by the trough; it was like a pond of mud by the time we got to it. We got covered in mud from head to toe by the other children shoving and pushing each other. I held the kettle whilst Charlie turned on the tap. It sent out a sudden gush of water, making me jump back in fright spilling water all over us. Charlie screamed at me, "Now look what you bin and done. Mum's gonna go mad when she sees us." Snatching the kettle, he refilled and dragged me back across the field, slopping water all over the place as we went.

"Whatever ave you two bin playing ?" said Mum, as she took the kettle from us. She was furious but my father just laughed.

"Don't keep on at em so, Mima," he said. "Don't keep on, it's just a drop of water, that's all."

"That's all!" she screamed. "How the hell am I gonna get the mud off em then, you tell me that."

Dad shook his head. "I don't know you two," he said with a sigh. "You bin and set your mother off agin, that's fer sure."

Dad began to tie up large bundles of wood; he then placed them in the corner of the hut.

"Wot you doin, Dad?" I asked. "Wot you making?"

Charlie laughed. "You don't know nothin," he said. "You're just a gel and they don't know nothing."

Dad shouted, "Leave her alone, Charlie, don't keep on at her so," Turning to me, he said, "I'm making a bed, Shill, that's all. We just gotta get some straw for it." He went off and returned a short time later with a big bail of straw on his back. Mum gave him a mattress cover she had made from two sheets. She and dad stuffed it with the straw. "There" he said, as she inspected it after throwing it onto the bavins of wood he had made. "Fit for a king, that is, and as warm as toast."

My mother made the bed, mumbling about us living like pigs, and getting our death of colds, whilst Dad just laughed at her. "You ave to moan, Mima," he said, "don't ya. You're not happy less'n you can moan about somethin."

It was getting dark now and almost everyone had moved in. My aunts, like my father, were happy to be there, and so were their husbands. It was just our mum that was unhappy about it all. People sat around their fires talking about what they had been up to during the year, as most of them only met at hop picking time. They had a lot to talk about.

"Time for bed," said Mum from our hut door way.

"Oh no, Mum," we pleaded, "can we stay up just a bit longer?"

"No," she said, "it's bed time for you two."

"Oh, let em stay up a bit longer, Mima," said Dad. "Its Sunday tomora, we don't start till Mundy, do we now."

"Time for bed, Sunday or not," she shouted back at him.

Dad smiled down at us and said, "Ya best go in for she blows her stack." Dad's relations laughed as we reluctantly went into the hut to our mother for bed.

EXPLORING

I woke up the next day to the sound of my father coughing. He had a very bad smoker's cough but still he smoked. He woke us up each morning with it. Mum was sorting out our clothes in the flickering candle glow. The hut was so cold that you could see your breath when you spoke. Hurriedly Mum dressed us then sent us out to Dad by the fire. The morning mist was low on the ground underneath the hedgerows. It came swirling across the field where Dad was feeding our old horse that had been tethered out in it. We could see the vapour from its mouth as it ate. Coming out of the hut, Mum bent down and stirred a big black pot that hung from an angle iron over the fire. Charlie and I crept closer to it, shivering in the cold morning air. Then, after a plate of steaming porridge and a cup of hot tea, my mother sent us for water, then we went off to explore.

We made our way over to the ramshackle brick building on the other side to look at the Londoners. They were not like us. They didn't even talk the same. Dad said that they spoke cockney. They fascinated me with the way they talked. They seemed to like us and we liked them. "Are you twins?" one of them asked.

"No, we ain't!" shouted Charlie. "I'm eighteen months older than she is."

"But you're so much alike," said the woman that had been speaking to us. "You look like twins." she reiterated.

"Well we ain't," Charlie replied, as he dragged me across the field towards the lavatory, if that's what you could call it. It was nothing more than a tin shed over a hole in the ground. There were no windows in it, just a door with a gap at the top and bottom of it. Inside was a long box over a hole in the ground with three round holes cut out on the top of it that you sat on, each round hole that much smaller than the other. It was dark inside so I made Charlie come in with me. I was afraid of spiders. Charlie took the greatest delight in pulling off their legs. It made me shiver when he did it and I ran out screaming. "Don't go wetting yourself," he shouted, "or I shall get the blame if you do."

I ran to Mrs Simms, the Londoner. She was nice to me and told Charlie off for teasing me. She said she would tell Mum of him if he did it again.

The Londoners never had their men with them like us. Their men only came at weekends as they worked in London and were not able to get the time off. Their women folk didn't mix well with us as they were wary of us. I don't think they knew how to take us as we had our own way of doing things.

PLAYING WITH FIRE

That night, we sat by the flickering fire light with Mum Dad and some of our relations. The sky was pitch black, except for the stars that seemed to wink at us. The moon was full and I could see a ring of light all around it. Charlie and I huddled closer together to keep warm. Dad was happy, we could tell. Leaning forward, he picked up a dying ember from the fire to light his cigarette. As he puffed at it, sparks flew off it and it glowed all red in the dark. "Them Woodbines will be the death of you, Charlie Ayres," Mum said.

Dad laughed at her. "Don't talk out the back of yer head, woman, don't talk such rot." We sat by the fireside, our eyes burning. Whether it was from the smoky fire or tiredness, I don't know, but I was finding it very hard to keep my eyes open. Dad got up. "Come on, Mima," he said. "Get the children to bed, we got work in the morning. We can't sit here all-night gabbing." So off we went to bed.

31

THE START OF A WORKING DAY

We woke up to the familiar sound of dad coughing. The hut was so cold. Charlie sat up in bed; he was blowing little puffs of vapour through his fingers. "Look, She," he said. "I'm smoking."

"Stop messing around and get dressed," said Mum, as she gave him a pair of short trousers that just about covered his knee caps. He then put on a liberty bodice and a flannelette shirt, over which he pulled on a thick woollen jumper. "Don't forget your coat," said Mum, holding out a coat towards him. Charlie put it on, and then a balaclava hat. All you could see was his face. I had fleecy drawers, a liberty bodice like Charlie, and over that a flannelette petticoat. My dress just covered my knees. Mum helped me on with my coat and she tied a woolly hat on my head. On our feet we had wellingtons and, on our hands, we wore socks for gloves. Outside dogs were sniffing about, picking up scraps of food that had been left by the fire the night before. They then lifted one leg and urinated, marking their territory on the hut door posts, the vapour rising from the urine in little spirals.

I could hear my aunts calling their children to get up, whilst their husbands sat drinking tea by their fires. People were milling around all over the place, lighting fires and making ready for the day ahead of them. Dad came back from feeding our horse and sat down. Mum made him some tea as he sat by the fire having a cigarette. She then went back into the hut to get our dinner bag ready for the day out in the hop fields.

Wandering back to our hut, we watched as she got our food. Dad came to the door. "ain't you ready yet, Mima," he asked.

"No, I'm not," she replied, "give me chance, man." I watched as she checked the bag once more. There was a tin kettle, a tin of condensed milk, sugar in a little cone of paper and a packet of tea. She then put in a loaf of bread wrapped in a clean tea towel. There was a half pound of butter as well as a piece of cheese. She then put in a bag of tomatoes. A box of jam tarts was next, then two cups a knife and a spoon. She then put in our Smiths Alarm clock.

Dad came back again. "Ain't you ready yet?" he shouted. "All the rest are ready to go except you, Mima."

"I'll come when I'm good and ready," she said, "so you hold yer horses. Don't rush me, man, or Ill forget something and that will be wrong as well." Putting her coat on and tying her head scarf under her chin, she emerged from the hut.

"About time, too," he said, as he kicked out the fire.

Other people were walking across the fields, our aunts and uncles in front, their children trailing behind them with bags and kettles, dogs yapping at their heels. We crossed the field and went down a steep slope that had little steps cut into it. My father was in front of us, bumping the old Tansad pram that we took to keep our things in out into the hop garden during the day, down each step-in front of him. Stinging nettles grew out over the path, stinging our legs where our wellingtons didn't quite reach. I cried and cried. Dad picked a dock leaf and put it on my leg. "There, that'll take the sting out," he said. The leaf felt cool on my leg as I wiped the tears from my eyes on my coat sleeve.

Mum gripped my hand tightly. "Stay by me and ya won't get stung," she said. I clung to her, I wasn't about to get stung again if I could help it, not me. Down the lane, past the forge, a sharp left and there were the cart tracks that went to the hop fields. The cart ruts were full of water as it had rained during the night.

Charlie and I walked in them, splashing water as we went. The going was hard and the mud squelched under foot. Mum kept on at us not to get wet. On our left were long rows of mangles and potatoes, and on the other was a field of stubble, because the corn had been cut. At the edge of it were two big ricks, and there was a crowd of boys jumping all over them. "Look at them boys," said Dad. "The man a have em locked up if he sees what they bin and done to them ricks." Taking off his trilby hat, he waved it angrily at them. "Get off that rick," he yelled, "before ya get locked up for it. Just look at the mess ya ave bin and made of it." The boys laughed at him before running off. We continued walking until we came to a brow of a small hill. Dad stood looking up at the clear blue sky. "Looks like a nice day," he said.

Mum sniffed, "Nice day indeed," she replied. "Just look at all this mud."

Dad gave her a side long glance and replied, "Don't go on, Mima, just take a look at that. ain't that a pretty sight for sore eyes and no mistake." He was talking as though he was seeing the view that he now held for the first time, although he had seen it year after year. He picked me up so I had a better view of it. I held my breath as the view was breathtaking. I think it's a sight that all young children should see. Nature at its best. The countryside stretched out before us, all shades of green and brown. Dad gave a deep sigh. He loved the countryside and no mistake. "It's just like a big patchwork quilt, ain't it." he said.

After some time, we came to a row of tall trees that had a hedgerow in front of them. The hedgerow was covered in wild honeysuckle and old man's beard.

To the right of that was a wood surrounding a small hop garden on three sides of it. I think it must have been planted in a crater, as it was like a huge hole. "That's bull pit," said Dad, putting me down. Turning from me, he walked a few paces and stopped in front of the tall trees, and stopped at the entrance of a big hop garden. There in front of me was a sight I shall never forget. Rows upon rows of hops as far as the eye can see. Hops grow on a bine; their cones are about as big as a marble although some can get as big as a plum. They grow up strings to a network of wires, which are supported by poles every now and then. The poles are about nine feet high, I think, and the leaves on the hops are rather like an oak leaf but bigger, with scratchy spines on the back of them. "This is the big hop garden," said Dad. "You ain't seen nothing like this before, ave ya, Shill." And indeed I must say that I hadn't.

Charlie and I ran down the long rows of hops, making tracks in the undisturbed chickweed that grew between them. We ran until our parents were out of sight, then raced back down the row towards them, pushing and shoving each other out of the way so as to be back first. People stood around; they were waiting for the whistle to blow. It was more than your job was worth to start without it, as to do so meant instant dismissal. There was a shrill sharp whistle and then crash, down came the hop bines at the top of each row, each hop picker trying to be the first to pull a bine. "I think we were the first this year, Mima," Dad said, then he laughed.

Mum shook her head. "I hate hopping," she said. "Me hair's all wet and me hands sting." Taking of her headscarf she ran her fingers through her thick black curls.

"Oh, don't start again, Mima," said my father. "Put some Vaseline on them, for Christ's sake, woman, and stop your moaning all the time." As the bine fell it covered Charlie and I with morning dew, its taste bitter from the hops. We could taste it in our mouths. Dad laughed as we spat it out. "You're soon get used to that," he said. "Give it a day or two." He was standing by my mother picking hops into a big basket that held five bushels when full. I could hear a scrunchy sound as they stripped the branches and leaves from the bine that was draped across the top of the basket. Mum kept putting her arms into the basket, heaping the hops up to the top of the basket. Dad laughed at her. "It's no good you keep on doing that," he said. "It won't make em any more than they are, you silly woman." The basket was just a little lower than me; I could just about see over the top of it.

Dad picked hops with Mum until about ten o'clock, and then he went off. He returned a short time later. "Soon be measuring time," he said. "I best be seeing if there's any hops caught on those top wires." Bending down he picked up a long pole, rather like a broom handle, but longer.

On the top was a hook like the letter r that had a sharp blade to the inside curve.

"What's that for?" I asked.

"This," he said "is a pole puller's hook. I'm a pole puller, ain't I. See up there," he said, laughing. "See them hops, they gotta come down."

There was a big bunch of hops hanging from the top wires. Dad raised his hook high in the air and, with a quick jerk of the wrist, he cut them down. "I don't want you two touching this," he said. "It'll cut yer fingers off. Now I better go before the governor blows his whistle and its blow-up time." He then disappeared down the row out of sight.

"It'll soon be time for the measure," said Mum, as she looked at the clock in the dinner bag. "I better get these hops in a poke, or I shan't get em measured when the men come to measure em. Go get me a poke, Charlie, and giv me an and to tip em up. Your father's never around when I need im." Charlie ran to the top of our row and returned with a big sack called a poke. Mum put the neck of the sack over the basket and she told Charlie to tip up his side. But Charlie was only small and the hops spewed out of the poke all over the ground. "Oh, that bloody man," Mum moaned. "Why is it he is never around when I need im. I'm better off doing it by myself."

THE MEASURERS

"I bet he's off gabbing to the men," she said. "Pole pulling, who do he think he's kidding." Just then the whistle went for the measure, and the measurers arrived at the top of our row with Mr Lane, the man in charge. Two men held the measuring bin whilst two more tipped in the hops from our poke at the end of the row. Mum stood nervously waiting for them to be done. Marking her card Mr Lane returned it. She gave a sigh of relief when he left. Dad sidled up to her and whispered in her ear. "I bet he throws them hops back at you, Mima, the next time," he said. "I was ashamed to look the man in the eyes when he measured our hops. I was too ashamed to look at him, I never seen so many stalks and leaves like you put in all the time. He's just refused one of the Londoner's hops because he said that they were dirty, full of stalks and leaves, and you go and do that."

Mum laughed "I gotta fill the basket somehow ,ain't I. I got to earn some money, you're never ere." Dad walked down the row mumbling to himself. Charlie was busy making a swing from a picked hop bine. He hung it from the wire that ran along the rows of hop bines, as they were supported by a wire that went the whole length of the row, about half way up. Taking off his coat, Charlie folded it and balanced it on the bine to make a seat and sat down. The wires squeaked as he swung to and fro and he went higher and higher. "Give me a go," I asked. "Give us a go."

"No, make your own," he said. "This one is mine."

Dad came back after the measuring for his dinner, so I asked him to make me a swing like Charlie's. "He's got a swing, Dad," I shouted.

"He better not be on them wires," Dad replied. "He knows I'll get the sack if the governor catches im on them."

Charlie sauntered down the row towards us a face a picture of innocence. "You bin on them wires boy?" Dad asked. "You know you'll be in for a thrashing if I catch yer on em."

Sitting down, Charlie leaned over towards me. "Big mouth, tale tit," he said. "Just because you ain't got one you had to split on me, didn't ya."

Mum was sitting by the fire she had made, blowing into it, cursing for all she was worth. "How I'm supposed to make tea I don't know," she said. "I can't get a kettle to boil let alone make tea."

"Get outta the way, woman," Dad said impatiently, "You make me sick. I can't even eat a bit of grub without your constant moaning all the time."

"Well you see if you're any better," she said. "You try and boil a kettle on that smoky old fire. Charlie and I sat quietly waiting for our dinner. We knew better than to say anything when they were having words.

Taking out our food from the bag, Mum spread it on a tea towel. Bread and cheese never tasted so good nor tomato so sweet, but we had to eat it with a piece of paper around it, as the hop stains on our hands made it taste bitter. If you didn't cover it, it was uneatable.

Then, after dinner, we ran to the top of the row and dived head first into the pokes of hops that were stacked at the end of it ready for the measurers. "I hope you're not jumping about on them hops," shouted Mum. "You'll make em go to powder and the foreman will be after ya."

THE TREK TO THE POST OFFICE AT THE END OF THE DAY

About half past four in the afternoon, my mother started to collect our belongings. "Come on," she said, "let's get going, it's time to make tracks." A long line of weary women and children made their way homeward to the huts. The muddy ground of the morning was now as dusty and dry as could be, covering our boots in a thick chalky film. Little gusts of wind sent it swirling into our faces, stinging our eyes. By the time we reached the end of the cart track we were covered. Some of the women turned to the right to go back to the huts, while the rest of us went to the little post office at the end of the village. The winding road stretched out before us, not much better than a cart track, its gravelled surface full of pot holes. At last we reached the post office; wearily we joined the queue to get served.

I loved that little shop as it smelt of all sorts of nice things to eat. Mum held onto her ration book; it was just the end of the war. There was still rationing.

Charlie and I stood in front of the counter peeping over the top. We were watching the man behind it cut our cheese. He was using a wire cutter on a board. His wife was using some little scales made of brass, putting little weights of brass on one side of her scales and apples on the other.

The man then took a pat of butter and two paddles. He began to pat the butter into a square before wrapping it in greaseproof paper. At the front of the counter there were boxes of biscuits on the floor. They had glass lids on them; we gazed at them longingly. Mum brought us the broken ones, as that was all she could afford. There were also big tins of Smiths crisps and boxes of apples. On the shelves were pots of homemade jam and packets of washing soda. Soap was cut off a long bar and they sold little blue bags that was used to put in the washing to make things look white. Mum asked for a box of candles and then gave the woman her ration book, as the man gave her a paper cone filled with sugar.

"You sure that's all?" said the man as he put it into Mum's bag for her.

"Yes, I can't afford no more," she said, "as much as I'd like it."

The man leaned over the counter and smiled at us. "My goodness, missus," he said, "they littluns ave growed." He ruffled my hair.

"Yes, they've grown up much too fast," she replied as she ushered us out the shop. As we left, we saw some of our cousins sitting on the shop wall outside. They sat there with legs dangling each side of the wall, trying to shove each other off. Charlie was itching to join them, but Mum gave him no chance. Back to the huts we trudged, tired and hungry.

On reaching the huts we flopped onto our bed, flat on our backs as we lay staring up at the ceiling. Mum called out to us to go get some water. She was busy making a fire. Aunt Louie had hers well alight and her dinner on the go. "I don't know how she does it," said Mum. "She's always the first to get her fire going."

Aunt Louie came over and said, "Take a fire brand from mine, Mima, and poke it into the middle, it'll catch light quicker."

"No, I can do it," said Mum obstinately.

Aunt Louie walked away saying, "All right, don't say I never offered to help yer. You'll never cook vittles on that."

Charlie and I went to get water for Mum, slopping it out as usual. By the time we got back our hands stung; the scratches on them began to smart once water came into contact with them. I cried and cried as Mum washed them in warm water. "I told yer not to play with them hops," she said. "Now perhaps you'll listen when I tell yer not to touch em." She began to cut up a sheet into strips to make bandages and she smeared our hands with Vaseline before wrapping them up. "There that's better," she said giving me a hug. "They'll harden up in a few days."

Dad returned with the men a short time later, starving hungry. "Come on, Mima, where's my grub?" he demanded.

Mum got up from the fire. "In the pot, old man, where do ya think it is?" she moaned.

"Ya mean to tell me that me grub's not done," he yelled. "What ave ya bin doing, woman?"

"Getting shopping and seeing to the kids," she said. "What else do ya think I've bin doing? I can't cook with all this smoke blinding me eyes." She began dabbing the smoke from them with the corner of her headscarf.

"I just offered to help her, Charlie," shouted Aunt Louie, "but she don't want my help. She's too much of a lady for that."

Mum glared at her, she kept herself to herself, and Dad's family didn't understand her at all. "Just because I won't go munging with yer sisters, they don't like me," she said to him. "I'm not knocking on doors with a basket on me arm like they do. My people don't do that."

"My people," said Dad, "who are they?"

She was furious with him. "Not hedge-mumpers like yours," she replied. "We got some pride."

Dad walked away. Mum had gone too far this time, but she had said it and would not take it back no matter what. She was so strong-willed at times. Once she put her foot down, that was that. The only thing she never got her way on was going hop picking.

The weeks passed very quickly, and it was soon time for us to return to our little bungalow back home. Mum was so happy. This time it was

Dad that had the long face on the return journey home. Mrs Wright was there to meet us, arms outstretched. Charlie wasn't too happy about it because he had to go to school and he hated it. This was to be the start of my wonderful hop picking holidays that I would remember for the rest of my life, and the start of many happy days.

THE NEW BABY

The year had passed by full of events, the biggest being the arrival of the new baby. The midwife came each day to Mum on her black bike until the baby arrived. Charlie said that it was in her black bag that was strapped on the carrier on the back of her bike. I waited patiently for her each day, asking her each time if she had my new baby in it. She just smiled and said, "No, not today dear."

Mum gave birth to a little boy with jet black hair and brown eyes. He was not at all like Charlie and me. Barry, as that is what Mum and Dad called him, was as dark as we were fair. People kept remarking on it. Mum was as proud as a peacock of him and we knew it. She just couldn't hide it. She also thought that my father would stay at home and not go hop picking now that she had the new baby. Dad had other ideas about it, he was going and that was that.

Barry was born in the July. "Charlie, I can't go," she protested. "I just can't."

"Of course you can,"Dad said. "Just wrap him up, he'll be all right."

Mum sat and cried while Mrs White tried to comfort her. "Don't cry, my ducks," she said. "He won't listen to me, I did try to talk him out of going but he just wouldn't listen." My mother packed our things as she had done the previous year, rather reluctantly.

Dad was in his element. "You're not the first woman to ave a baby. Look at Carrie and Louie, they ad babies and it never made no odds to them."

"I'm not Louie," shouted mum. "I'm me." Dad just laughed at her, so it was useless for her to argue with him. He had been hopping since he was a baby, so he wouldn't stop, no matter what. The only year he missed going was in 1941, the year that I was born, and then, only because mum had been confined to bed. He never let her forget it for one moment.

We made our way to Binstead the same as the previous year by horse and cart, Mum sitting up front with the baby in her arms, crying as she waved to Mrs White. Charlie and me sat singing on the back of the cart, as happy as larks. All the way there Mum fretted over the baby and when we went over the hog's hill back, she begged Dad to stop and let us get off the cart. She thought the horse would fall down on its knees and we would all fall out.

Dad laughed and laughed. "You cranky woman," he said. "I'm not stopping, who ever heard of such a thing," Later on, he told Aunt Louie about it in the pub; she laughed as well at Mum. Dad's family talked about her enough, she knew they did. Ever since she'd married my dad, they held a grudge, or so she thought.

To explain, Mum had been going out with my father's brother, Henry, before Dad. Henry was in the army and Dad had swiped Mum from him as she thought he no longer loved her. Our aunts really never forgave her for it, or Henry when he returned, as it caused a rift between the two brothers. They didn't speak to each other for years because of it. Besides all this my mother didn't even dress like them. She refused to wear the plaid skirts and black aprons like they did, and to top it off she refused to have her ears pierced.

After arriving and getting the water we ran off to explore. I don't know what we expected to find but off we went anyway. The place was just the same as the previous year, Londoners one side of the field and us the other. The big boys raced around the field with their dogs, Jacky and Mushy taunting each other's dog. "Get im, get im," Mushy shouted to his dog as he grabbed at his cousin's jacket. The dog ran around snapping and snarling nipping at Jacky. My cousin Albert joined in as well. Aunt Louie came out of her hut and saw them. Picking up a stick from a bavin she gave chase. Mushy never saw her until she gave him a hefty clout with it. Jacky and Albert laughed and then smack, she gave them one also. "I'll teach you to make them dogs bite," she yelled. "You'll get locked up for it." Dragging them back to the hut, she gave them one last whack around the ear before letting them go. It did not matter to her that they were not her children; she hit them just the same. She dished out food and discipline when needed.

The men sat around the fire bragging about their dogs and horses to each other whilst their woman folk got the children to bed. Dad loved it as he could be with his brothers and sisters for at least a month. Dad was the baby of the family and he so missed their company, especially his sister, Louie, as she had taken a big part in his upbringing. My grandmother lived with Louie after the death of her husband, Joe Ayres. She still called our dad her baby. She loved all her children about her. My Uncle Joe and Uncle Henry were the only two children missing.

Granny Tilda and Aunt Louie sat by the fire combing out their long waist length hair and then replaiting it. They then pinned it into two coils at the back of their heads. Louie's brother, Jim Lane, began to sing as he played two spoons up and down his leg. "Diddle I dy dy diddle I dy dy." He sang and Dad clapped in time to the tune. Aunt Louie and Aunt Carrie linked arms and began to dance, swinging each other around. The fire spat sparks in every direction as the two of them danced.

"Come on, Mima," shouted Dad. "Come out here."

"I ain't got time," she said. "I got a baby to see to. I ain't got time to mess around dancing." This year was very hard for Mum. She got so tired at the end of the day and washing the baby's nappies was a nightmare. She hated the nights as Dad went to the pub, leaving her all alone at the huts, frightened stiff listening to every sound. Our dog sat at the hut door on guard. It was the only time that she would allow it in. Sometimes she would take us to the pub to sit outside on the steps waiting for Dad to come home. "Please come home, Charlie," she begged. "The children are cold and tired."

"Can't yer leave im alone," said Aunt Louie. "Can't yer leave a man alone to ave a drink in peace?"

Mum told her that she should mind her own business and she should keep out of it. "I'm not stopping at them huts night after night on my own," she said. "I can't even lock a door."

Dad and Aunt Louie laughed. "Who's gonna ert you?" said Dad. "Who do ya think's at the huts? You never see them Londoner women complain. They ain't got no men with them, ave they. Take the kids home. I'll be home later." In the end mum stopped going to the pub for him, as it was just a waste of time to do so.

Sometimes, during the day, Indians wearing turbans came to the hop fields. They sold all sorts of ribbons, kerchiefs and pure silk night dresses. Uncle Jim Lane brought a kerchief and some red ribbons from them. Later that night as I sat on my father's knee by the fire, I watched my uncle put on his new kerchief around his neck. "Come on Celia," he said, "come and see what I got off the black man fer yer." My Uncle Jim always called me Celia as it was his sister's name and he said I reminded him of her. He held out a bright red ribbon towards me. "Come and let your Aunt Louie plait yer hair and ya can ave it," he said. As I sat on his lap, my aunt made two stumpy plaits.

"There," she said, as she tied them together with the red ribbon. "You're a proper little gypsy girl now. All yer need is yer ears pierced." She took a needle and cork from her pocket. "Yer won't feel it," she said, "and when your holes heal up your Uncle Jim's gonna buy you some gold sleepers to put in. We'll put a bit of cotton in them fer now."

I jumped up in fright. "No no," I shouted. "I don't want needles in me ears."

Dad laughed. "You can't feel it," he said. "It won't urt." I wasn't about to see if it did or not. I ran to our hut to see my mother. She wouldn't let them touch me; I knew she wouldn't.

Mum was very angry. "Fancy frightening the child like that," she said to Dad as she undid my hair. "I don't want her ears pierced. When I do, I'll ask, and it won't be with a needle and cork, that's for sure."

The time soon passed by and we returned to our homes once more, all in different places. A sad little band made its way homeward, sure of just one thing, and that was that we would all meet again the following year.

PLAYING WITH FIRE

After arriving at the huts this year, we did the usual things then settled in. Mr Lane came over to my aunts and told them to keep a tight rein on the boys. He said that he would sack any one that damaged farm crops like they did last year; he said that he would not tolerate it any more. My Aunt Louie assured him that she would keep a closer eye on the children. She assured him that they would not go coursing with the dogs on farm land. "Miserable old sod," she said to Dad as Mr Lane walked away. "He's always gotta find somthin to ave a moan at."

Dad laughed at her. "Yer better do as he says, you'll get the sack if'n yer don't."

"No, he won't," she replied. "He can't do that, he wouldn't dare do that."

"Can't he?" said Dad. "I wouldn't be too sure of that, if I was you."

Mr Lane was a small man with a hook nose. I think he was Jewish, he certainly looked Jewish. He always dressed in dark chequered suits and a cloth cap. The hops had to be just right or he would not take them. Mum was all right with him, though, as I think he thought she was of Jewish descent. She could easily be mistaken for one, with her coal black hair and mass of curls. She also had dark brown eyes and a rather big nose. Dad laughed at her. "It's no good you keep smiling at im, Mima, trying to butter I'm up. It won't work, yer know. You'll cop it just the same as the rest of us if'n yer keep putting in all those stalks and leaves like yer do." Dad went on. "He's just refused one of the Londoner's hops because he said that they was dirty."

Mum didn't care, she just smiled at him when he came to measure our hops and said, "Nice day, Mr Lane." He would smile back at her and touch his cap in reply. No matter how many leaves and stalks she put in the basket, he never refused to take them.

One night, we sat by the fire side poking in the ashes for our baked potatoes, elbowing each other out of the way in an attempt to get at them.

51

My grandmother, Matilda, sat by the fire. She was peeling vegetables for tea into a large bowl on her lap, nodding off as she did so. My Aunt Louie called out from her hut doorway. "Keep an eye on em, mother," she said, "just while I throw up the beds. Watch em by the fire for me." Granny nodded in reply, her old grey plaits falling as she did so.

My cousin, Tillie Lane, stuck a stick in her potato. It was all black and had bits of hot ash still clinging to it. Her brother, Johnny, started to push and elbow his way in when, all of a sudden, she fell on her bottom. I don't know quite what happened next, but all hell broke loose. Tillie took off across the field as it the devil was after her, screaming for all she was worth.

Tillie ran towards the men that were out in the field feeding their horses. By the time they realised what had happened to her she was hysterical. As they removed the wellington boot from her foot, so the skin came away with it. Tillie was rushed to hospital and the rest of us given a lecture from granny, as she had now woken up.

Later that night, my mother took Charlie and me to one side, and she impressed upon us the danger of fire. "Don't play with fire, and yer won't get burnt," she said. My cousin, Tillie, was left with a scar the length of her shin bone. The hot potato had fallen down inside her boot. It had rolled all the way down her shin and lodged itself at the bottom.

THE P.O.W. MEN (Prisoners of war)

Just behind our huts there was a potato field. Prisoners of the war were set to work in it, along with some of the villagers, picking up potatoes. We children often sat on the stile to watch them. They waved at us and sometimes, they walked over to us to talk. We never understood their language as they spoke German. On one such occasion Aunt Louie caught them. She boxed our ears and shouted at them to go away. "Don't ever let me catch yer talking ta them men," she said. "Them lot ave bin killing our boys."

"What do ya mean Aunt Louie?" I asked.

"They're bad men and I don't want ter ever catch yer talking to em again."

Bad men I thought to myself, what did she mean? They gave us their sweets and picked us up when we fell off the stile. They even rubbed our knees. So how was it that they were such bad men? I didn't understand grown-ups at times.

Another hop picking season was at an end and we were packing our things once more to return to our homes. The weeks had passed by so quick, it had seemed to me.

On arrival back home we soon settled in once more. Our bungalow wasn't anything special, but to us it was home. Charlie was in trouble when he went back to school as he could neither read or write. I wasn't doing too well either. I couldn't do anything as I had missed the first stages of learning and I couldn't grasp even the simplest of things. Dad didn't worry too much about it, he had other things on his mind to worry about. Work was hard to come by and it took all his time to find a job. Mum thought that she had a weapon to use against him now to not go hopping, as the education authorities were on his back. Dad didn't care.

"They can't do nothin, Mima," he said, "can they now. They can't stop me from taking my children away on holiday."

Shaking her head, she walked away. Even though my mother could read and write very well, she never had the time to teach us. Mum had lost again; Dad always had an answer for everything.

THE DONKEY

When we were not in school, we spent most of our time in the yard as we had so many animals to look after. Our backyard was more like a farmyard than a garden. We had ducks, chickens, rabbits, pigs. One time, Dad bought us a donkey. Mum hated it. "I don't know why yer wasted yer money on that useless thing," she said. "It's an old nag."

Dad laughed at her as he always did. "You talk rot, Mima," he said. "I brought this fer the kids to ride, and fer Christ's sake, stop moaning, woman. all yer ever do is moan."

The donkey was useless to ride as it bucked us straight off. Mum went mad. "I bet you'll kill them kids, Charlie Ayres," she said. "Then you'll be satisfied, I know." She went on so much that my father sold it. Boy was he mad when the donkey had a foal the very next day. I thought he was going to kill Mum.

"That'll teach yer to listen to Mima," said Aunt Louie. "You should

be a man of yer own house, and not let the woman dictate what yer can and can't do." Mum and she had words over it, they almost came to blows. This didn't last though. They had a habit of rubbing each other up the wrong way, but they didn't seem to hold malice.

THE ROUGH GYPSIES

This year when we went hop picking at Hay Place farm it would be with Dad's brother, Albert, as our aunts had been told not to bother coming back. I think it was because of their sons' persistence in going coursing on the farm land that did it. They had to go to another farm this time. It was Lilly White's at the other end of the village. It was just past the post office. My mother's sister, Ivy, was to go with them for some reason or other. So that only left Aunt Liza and Uncle Albert.

Mr Lane came over to Dad. He asked him to move over to the huts by the old ramshackle cookhouse. "The wife won't be lonely over there," he said. "There's more to keep her company over that side, Charlie." Dad reluctantly agreed and we moved our things in over the other side. We were just like fish out of water for the first few days, but Mum soon got to like talking to the Londoners, and after a while so did Dad. There was just one thing that spoilt it for us and that was the gypsies.

A crowd of really rough gypsies had made camp over the far side of the field. They were just in the corner, up against the orchard fence. What a rough lot they were. Dad called them hedge-mumpers. They were always fighting and they made their surroundings a dump. I had the feeling that Mr Lane felt that we were too vulnerable on the other side on our own and that was the reason he suggested that we move. "They say we are bad," said Mum. "At least we wash and comb our hair, we ain't like that lot."

Just with all races, there was a degree of hierarchy in the gypsy world. Dad told Mum to keep quiet. "Yer don't want no trouble with the likes of them. They will take the eyes from yer head as soon as look at yer," he said.

They kept scrawny, mangy dogs that were on the scrounge for food all the time and they constantly fought over it. We returned to the huts one day to find we had been broken into. Mum's washing was missing, pegs and all. I was so upset as I had my new dresses on the line. It wasn't all that often that I had new things as Mum could not afford them. Most of my clothes were from my aunt, as she was often given children's clothes when she went calling. I was to see one of my dresses a few days later. It was on one of the gypsy girls. "That's my dress," I said. "Get it off, I know it's mine."

"No," said the girl, "it's mine."

"No, it ain't," I yelled. "Give it back."

Laughing at me, she wiped her dirty hands on it.

Running in to our hut I called my mother. "Mum, Mum, that girl's got my frock on."

"Yes, I've seen her," she replied.

"Well tell he to take it off then," I yelled. "Tell err its mine."

"No," said Mum. "She will tell her father and that lot a be over here to yer Dad. That lot would slit yer throat as soon as look at yer, they would. No, you don't say nothing to her." To see her prance around in my dress was all I could stand at times. The owner had so many complaints about them that he had to tell them to go in the end. How happy everyone was when we watched them leave. They stole quite a few things before they finally went. They took all our wood for fire and a big sack of potatoes as well. The carter had to get us some more the next day.

BARRY

Out in the hop garden every day, our Barry sat playing in his pram as happy as could be, as long as he could see Mum. She had put various things in his pram to play with. She even threaded some milk bottle tops across the pram so as he could play with them. Charlie and I found various things to do, one being that we would roll around in an empty hop basket until Mum caught us. "Yer father left that fer yer to put hops in, not smash to bits," she said. "You'll cop it when he gets back, you see if ya don't." She put her hand in her pocket and she took out a barley sugar sweet. "The one that picks the most hops gets the most sweets," she said. "Come on, yer best pick somethin before yer dad gets back." Charlie often went off on his own, leaving me to pick by myself. Mum stopped from time to time to see to Barry. She simply adored him.

The Londoners laughed at her. "He ain't like the otha two, Mima" they said.

"I don't know what you bin up to," said Mrs Simms, "he's nothing like them." Barry was as dark as we were fair, he had two of the biggest dimples, one in each cheek and Mum's dark eyes. His hair stood on end like a black brush. "Just look at them eyes," said Mrs Simms. "They're as black as Sloes."

Dad came back. "Put him down, Mima," he said. "You'll ruin im if yer don't." He went on, "You keep picking im up all day, woman."

"I shan't," she said. "I gotta feed im, ain't I."

"You pamper I'm too much," said Dad. "You'll be sorry for it one of these days, you see if you ain't."

Mum just laughed at him as she continued to play with my brother.

Charlie and I thought we would go and see what was going on at the top or our row of hops. We never went too far from Mum and Dad, we were never allowed to. We ran through the rows, swinging on the wires as we went, jumping over the mounds of earth in between each row. We stopped at the end and stood looking at the wood that faced us. Blackberries and wild sloe fruit grew at its edge and it looked dark and foreboding inside. Mum called out to us, "Don't you go in them woods. There's nasty men in there and they'll take little boys and girls away," she shouted. We stood eating berries and sloe fruit until we were sick. They gave us stomach ache.

EXPLORING

Forgetting my mother's warning, Charlie and I ran off to explore. Charlie took me to a big gate and we sat on top of it. "Look, She," he said. "I can see the trains from here."

I climbed up beside him. "I can't see," I said.

"Look over there, you crank," he replied. "Can't yer see the smoke?" Straining my eyes, I just caught a glimpse of it as it disappeared behind the trees. "Bentley station's over there," he said. "It's just behind the trees."

There were cows in the field and so were the hop pickers' horses. Ours was over in the far corner. How long we sat there I don't know, but the next thing we heard was the jingle of the horse's harness as the cart came down the hill towards us. We raced up the hill towards it, jumping in and out of the cart ruts.

The carter was pulling back at the reins. "Whoa there, Blossom," he said. "Whoa, Boxer, whoa," as he fought to control them. The horses were pulling back at the reins, snorting and stamping their feet impatiently. The sweat glistened on their backs in the heat of the midday sun. They twitched and swung their heads from side to side to remove the flies that circled their heads. There were men piling up pokes of hops on the back of the cart.

Our father was with them. On seeing us he shouted, "Get out of the way and get back to yer mother at once." We ran off fast as we could, stumbling over the mounds of earth as we went. We knew that Dad was angry with us by the tone of his voice. When at last we got back to Mum, she was on her hands and knees blowing into the useless fire she had made, but all it did was smoulder.

Her face was black with smoke, her eyes streaming. She wiped the tears from them on her scarf and said, "I hope yer know yer dad's looking for you two. You'll cop it when he gets back, just you see if yer don't. You know ya ain't supposed to run off."

Charlie and I looked at each other; we knew we had done wrong. Dad was angry when he got back, but he soon forgot about it. He never stayed cross with us for very long.

There were talks of a new foreman. "Old Lane's going," said Dad to Mum. "I hear say that one of the farm workers is gonna take over."

"Who?" my mother asked.

"The feller with the two boys," he replied. "The one with the woman in glasses."

"What, them that live up Thurston's?" Mum said.

"Yes," said Dad. "I don't know how true it is, though."

"Well fancy that," Mum replied. "I never thought that old Mr Lane would go."

"As long as he's a fair man." Dad said. "I don't care who takes over as long as he is a fair man."

"What's he like?" asked Mum.

"How the hell should I know?" replied Dad.

"You work with him, don't ya?" she said.

"What a man's like to work with is not the same as working for him, not the same at all," he replied. Dad shook his head. "Women, they think they know it all," he said.

I think Dad missed his brothers and sisters not being at the farm this year, as he was only able to see them at the weekends. They still went to the White Hart and had a drink with him on Saturdays, but it was not the same as when they picked with him at Paul's farm, somehow. He had old man Keary to talk to and Ernie Steelwell, but he liked to talk to his own family. It was nothing to see him searching through his pockets for dog ends at the end of the week, when his money had run out. Mum would laugh at him and tell him that he would be better off not smoking. He just grunted and stormed off out. The little he got from his pole pulling job, just covered the food bill. There wasn't much left to get anything else for that matter.

CHARLIE AND THE NUT TREES

The next day my mother sent Charlie and me for wood for the fire. "Yer father's not got any wood," she said. "You two will have to go and get some. I shan't be able to boil the kettle without any wood. Look after her, Charlie, don't go too far, and don't go leaving her by herself."

Off we ran, before she had a change of heart. It was like a whole new world to me as we entered the wood. The trees rustling and wood pigeons cooing to each other were so peaceful. Our feet sunk into the damp leaves as we walked; it was almost like walking on air except a twig would snap every now and then and little streams of light sifted through the branches of the trees as they moved in the breeze. To me this was pure magic because if there such things as fairies, this was just the place to find them.

Charlie picked up wood whilst I filled the kettle from the little stream that meandered through the wood. Looking up I found that I was alone. "Charlie," I shouted, "Where are ya? Don't leave me alone. I'm telling Mum when I get back."

Charlie swung down from a tree a short distance from me. "You big baby," he said. "Just look at yer."

"Mum said not to leave me,, I replied. "You know she did."

"Who's gonna hurt ya?" he shouted. "One look at you and they'd run a mile."

"What about you then," I shouted back at him. He quickly climbed another tree, edging his way out onto a thin branch, then slowly made his way along it. Dropping to the ground, he clung onto it and shouted, "Well, pick the nuts, ya crank. I can't hold on all day, ya know."

I picked the nuts as fast as I could, stuffing them in my pockets. Charlie then let go of the branch, and swish, it went back into the air. "Give me my nuts," he demanded. "Hand em over."

"Can I have some?" I asked.

"No," he replied. "They're mine, not yours."

"I picked em, didn't I?" I asked.

"I got up the tree," Charlie shouted back at me. "So, give em ere." He ransacked my pockets for the nuts. I ran from the wood crying, completely forgetting the wood mother had sent us for. Charlie ran after me. asking me to come back.

I can still picture my mother's face when I got back. She stood with her hands on her hips. "Where's the wood?" she asked curtly, as Charlie caught up with me, puffing and panting out of breath. He stood, water dripping down his legs where he had spilt it running after me.

"We ain't got none," he shouted. "Sheila got lost and I ad ter go and find her," he lied. "She ran off, Mum."

"Liar, liar," I yelled. "He ran off to go nutting, Mum, he went off and left me. Look, he's got pockets full."

"You wait until yer father gets back, young man," she said. "You'll cop it. I can't trust you to do nuthin, can I? I should ave ad more sense than to send you two."

Charlie sat cracking nuts and eating them all day long, and when I

asked for one, he said, "No, you got me a clout so you can go without."
Digging me in the ribs. he said, "You opened yer big mouth, you ain't
getting none."

THE CART HORSES

The following night, Charlie and me were sent to get Mum's water. We wandered across to the barn. I can still see Old Bill, the carter's, face as we approached him. "Hello you, little uns," he said, in his gruff country voice. His red face was beaming and his eyes twinkling. He was standing by the water trough dressed in an open neck shirt and corduroys. On his feet he had hob nailed boots. Pushing his cap to the back of his head, he wiped it with his hand. We followed him into the stables. "You can watch em be fed," he said. "They don't bite if'n they be fed." He roared with laughter. The smell of oats and barley was strong as we stood by the stalls. There were three horses in them, Boxer, Diamond, and Blossom. Bill turned to us and said, "Do yer want ter get the feed out for un, do ee?"

The horses were swishing away the flies with their long tails, munching away at the hay in the racks in front of them. They gave a snort every now and then as they pawed the ground with their hooves. "I'll feed em," Charlie cried. "I will, Bill."

"Come on then," said Bill. He turned towards the grain box just inside the stable door. There were two lids on top of it. Opening one of them, Bill took out a big scoop. "One o they, lad" he said, "Not too much, mind, or they be frisky." Bill worked away on them with a curry comb in one hand and a brush in the other. He brushed and combed their coats until they shone.

After they had been fed, he took them out to the water trough one by one for water. The trough was on the left of the stable door just under the stable window. As Bill turned on the tap at the end of the trough it filled with water and the horse sucked and sucked at the water. I never thought it would stop. "Whoa, old girl," said Bill. "Don't drink it all, gal." He took the horse by its head harness and turned it away from the water. Smiling down at me, he asked, "Yer want a ride on ee?"

I stood rooted to the spot. "No no," I replied backing away.

"I will, I will," shouted Charlie. "Give us a go, Bill."

Bill turned to me once more. "Yer can get on ee if yer want, gal," he said. "They won't urt ee, gentle as lambs they be." He chuckled to himself. I shook my head; I liked the horses but not that much. The sheer size of them frightened me stiff. Bill lifted Charlie onto the big cart horse's back and held him by his jacket.

"Oh, She," he said, "it ain't arf high up here." He looked a little nervous to me, although he would never admit it.

"That's it,"said Bill. "I'll get the sack if the governor catches me giving you rides." He lifted Charlie down from the horse. "Go on, that's all, be off with ee" he said. "I'm gonna have a farm when I gets older bill I am," said Charlie. "I am, Bill and I'm gonna have horses and pigs and cows, I am."

Bill laughed. "You'll ave to grow a lot bigger than you are now, young un, and do yer book learning."

Charlie shouted, "No, I won't, I ain't ever going back to school ever again. I'm never going back."

"I think yer father'll ave somthin to say about that," said Bill, as he went back into the stables. "Oh, and I don't want you littluns in my cart shed or the stables when I'm not ere," said Bill, "and no going up in the hay loft the floor is rotten as a pear. Ya can get urt up there."

Charlie and I watched as he cleaned out the stalls. He threw buckets of water across a cobbled floor and swept it into a gully under the stable door. He then cleaned the horse harness. We wandered into a little room at the end of the stables. There were all sorts of harnesses hanging on the walls and some were on a bench at the back. Charlie liked the blinker, that's a harness with eye pads. But I liked the big head collars that hung from the walls as they smelt of leather and horses. They were padded and they had brass rings to them that the harness was attached to. Charlie followed Bill all over the place asking all sorts of questions as I stood by the door nervously watching him. I liked the horses but was afraid of them.

"These old horses won't urt ee on purpose, they won't," said Bill. "Gentle as lambs they be." He again began to chuckle as he spoke. "Yer best be of now afor thee mother gets to fretting over ee."

We filled the kettle at the trough and then went back to Mum. She was very angry with us for being so long. Hop picking was almost at an end and we would soon be going home again, although we were going to move to a new house this time, as we had been given a new house in Hersham.

70

THE NEW HOUSE

We moved into our new house full of excitement. That was, until we found out that we could no longer keep animals. They said that the only thing we could keep was a dog and we no longer had one. How the neighbours stared as we unpacked our things. "Just as good as them," said Mum, "if not better." The house was lovely but the garden seemed so small after the one we had when we lived in Field Common Lane. I missed the silver birch trees that grew at the end of our home, and I missed all of our animals as we had been used to keeping all sorts of livestock.

The reason we moved was because the rats kept getting into our bungalow. No matter how much poison Dad put down, they still came in. They came from the pig farm at the bottom of our garden. My mother had to send our clothes to the council, to a Mr Bevan, before we got re-housed. She sent him our clothes so that he could see they had been eaten by rats. Mum told him that she thought us children would be attacked in our sleep. She was given a house in a matter of weeks after that.

It meant we had to change schools as well. I was not going to like that at all as I was used to going to school with my brother. My brother was to be in a different playground to me, as this school had a different playground for boys. I could only see him through a spiked railing fence. The new children called me names and would not sit next to me, as I had no uniform. The teachers were not much better, either, as once they knew that I had come from Field Common, they didn't want to know. They couldn't be bothered with me. It didn't matter to them that I couldn't read. To them I was just a gypsy, an inconvenience, as far as they were concerned. They treated me like dirt.

You should have seen our neighbour's faces as we left to go to Binstead that year. I don't think that they had seen anything like it before. My Uncle Horace came to take us this year as we no longer had our horse and cart. Dad didn't have a place to keep it. We had to cram all our things in with theirs. We sat in the back with Aunt Ivy and her children, amongst the packing boxes.

Mum hated it. "Look at the neighbours, Charlie," she said. "I feel a proper fool."

Dad just laughed as he always did. "Look at em," he said. "It makes no odds to me."

Some of the children from our street asked us where we were going. "Hop picking," we shouted, "we're going hopping."

All the way there, Aunt Ivy kept on at us to not lean out of the cart. We felt thoroughly fed up by the time we reached the huts. Dad had to tell her to shut up in the end. "For Christ's sake ,Horace," he said ."She's bin an give me a bad head. She's enough ter send yer off yer head," he said. Ivy was my mother's sister but she, unlike my mum, loved hop picking. She would go on so as she was a bit deaf, I think, because she shouted all the time at you when she spoke.

Aunt Ivy's husband, Horace, was always drunk. He spent all of their money that they got from hopping on drink. He asked for a sub when their money ran out, so it was nothing for them to return after hop picking with no money. Uncle Horace had subbed it all during the four or five weeks that it had taken to pick the hops.

On our arrival this year we saw the same people that had been the previous year. The Steelwells had the black chicken hut and a woman called Eileen and her son had the shepherd's hut that stood in the field. The Londoners were all unpacking their few bits and pieces, doing as much as they could before their men folk had to return to their jobs in London.

PIG ON A STRING

Dad spoke to some of the men. "Don't go fretting about the women," he said. "Me and Mima will keep an eye on em fer yer. I'll look after em if they need anything." The men thanked him. Dad sorted out the hut with Mum as Charlie and I got water for her. Mum was so happy this year as she had her sister, Ivy, back to keep her company.

Our aunt had returned to our farm this year as she did not like the other farm that she had gone to with Dad's sisters. The Steelwells that stayed in the black chicken hut had a son called Dennis. Dennis and my little brother, Barry, became firm friends and went everywhere together.

Dennis had a little piglet which he took with him everywhere he went. The pig had been the runt of a litter of pigs and its mother had rejected it. Dennis had been put in charge of feeding it so he became its surrogate mother. What a strange sight they made, Barry, Dennis and that pig on a piece of string trailing behind them.

ROSE SMITH

This year, Mum's best friend, Rose, was to come with us. Rose was unable to afford a holiday this year for her children, so Dad and Mum persuaded her to come hop picking with us. Dad was so glad she was coming as he thought it would stop my mother from moaning. He didn't know our Aunt Ivy was to also return to Hay Place Farm again. All went well the first day, but the second day it rained all day long.

We all got well and truly soaked. Aunt Rose, as that is what we children called her, got wet through. She stayed at her basket nonetheless. She worked just as hard as the rest of us. The rain ran down her face and the headscarf stuck to her head. Dad laughed at her but she took no notice of him at all. She was determined to earn as much money as she could to take home to Uncle Dick, her husband, as he had not long come home from a prisoner of war camp. She had received a letter from the ministry saying that he was missing in action and he was presumed dead. A while after receiving the letter, Aunt Rose had met another man and was about to marry him when she got news that Uncle Dick was alive and in a prisoner of war camp. She was expecting a baby by the man she was about to marry. She called off the wedding and had to face Uncle Dick and tell him about the baby, when he eventually came home. Dick took on the child as if he were his own and treated him just the same as his own children.

When we got back to the huts that night, we all dried off as best we could. The Londoners laughed when they saw Aunt Rose, as her face was as red as a beetroot. The next day her head was so swollen and her eyes almost shut. Her hands were all blotchy as well and swollen. "I ain't never seen nothing like it," said Dad. "It must have bin the dye from her headscarf that's done it."

Rose went to see the doctor at Bentley. He gave her some medicine to take and he said she was to stay at the huts, and not go out in the hop fields and pick. It was no use, though. She became very ill and had to be taken home. Mum was so upset when she went, as were the rest of us. Aunt Rose was allergic to the hops and was to never be able to come hop picking ever again.

THE RABBITS

Mum's brother, Freddy, came down for the weekend. Dad and Uncle Fred went to the market on Saturday and they returned with some rabbits. "A nice drop of broth," said Dad, "nice rabbit stew."

Mum thought him quite mad and she said so. "What the hell are ya gonna keep em in?" she asked. "Who ever heard of keeping rabbits in a place like this with no hutch?"

Dad laughed at her. "You'll see," he said. "You'll see who's the crank when I knock one on the back of the head and lay it on the table for yer. You won't laugh then," he said, "will yer." He made a hutch from two orange boxes and some chicken wire. The door hinges were made from little strips of rubber inner tube from a bike wheel he had found. "There," he said as she inspected it. "That's what yer call a rabbit hutch."

Mum laughed. "The foxes will get em, you see if they don't, and if they don't someone else will."

Well, our rabbits didn't last long I can tell you. We lost them one by one. "I told yer they wouldn't last in a place like this," said Mum. "But yer wouldn't listen, would yer."

Our Uncle Fred came back the following weekend, and he and Dad sat talking. I don't know quite what was said, but Dad laughed. He told me and Charlie not to feed the rabbit that was left.

"Why can't we?" I asked. "What's wrong?"

"I know," said Charlie, there's ferrets in the hutch. I heard Uncle Fred tell Dad."

I stood on tiptoe and peered in. Sure enough, they were not rabbits at all but long cream things with little beady eyes. "If yer touch em they'll bite yer fingers off," said Charlie, his eyes getting bigger as he spoke.

"I thought I told you two not to touch the rabbits or feed them," said Dad. "I thought I told yer to keep away from em and not go near that hutch." We ran off as fast as we could. We didn't want to get a clout from Dad.

That night we heard a right din. "Somebody's found the rabbits, Mima," Dad said, laughing fit to burst.

"Yer never put the ferrets in with the rabbits, did yer?" she asked, knowing full well that he had. We didn't have any more taken but we lost them just the same.

Uncle Fred brought Mum's brother, Jimmy, to stay for a few days holiday. He wasn't a very bright boy and he had been brought up in an institution. It was called Bottley's Park, and being in a place like that was enough to send anyone off their head. Jimmy was quite happy until he saw the hops. He stood out in the hop garden looking up at the rows, his eyes filled with dismay. "Mima," he said, "it'll take forever to pick all this lot." He thought that you picked them one at a time. He didn't know that you stripped the leaves from the branches before they went in the bin.

Mum laughed, but Dad got mad with him and said, "If yer ain't gonna pick, go back to the huts. We got work to do, we gotta make a living." Jimmy couldn't go quickly enough.

"Oh, Charlie," said Mum, "yer don't have to shout at im like that, do yer. He don't understand."

"Any fool can pick a hop," said Dad. "It don't take much of a brain fer that, he's just idle that's all."

That night, when we returned to the huts, we found a gruesome sight.

All our rabbits were dead, the hutch filled with blood. "Somebody's gone and put the ferrets in with the rabbits,"said Dad. "Whoever done a thing like that?"

"I did," shouted Jimmy. "I thought they were lonely so I put them with the rabbits to keep em company."

"You cranky boy," shouted Dad. "Get outta my sight," he said, "or I'll kill yer." Dad was so angry with him. "Whoever heard of putting rabbits with ferrets, whatever next."

Jimmy was sent home the next weekend when our Uncle Fred came down. "Take away that cranky boy for I kill im," said Dad "I want im outta my sight." Uncle Fred laughed and laughed until he cried when Dad told him what Jimmy had done. Mum had a little laugh as well, but not in front of my dad as he was so angry.

Soon we were packing to go home once more. Mum was so happy and we were miserable. Home meant just one thing to me and that was school. Oh, how I hated it. Schooldays were supposed to be the happiest days of your life, but to me they were the worst.

When we got home that year, we found that all Charlie's racing birds had been stolen, and the pigeons they didn't take they killed. He was that upset when he saw what had happened to them. He had asked his friend, Alan Rutherford, to look after them while he was away, "And they reckon we're bad," said Dad to Mum. "At least we don't go around doing things like that."

Alan said that they had been fine the night before when he fed them. We found out who it was but it was no consolation to my brother, as he had been breeding his racing pigeons for some time. He had quite a few good birds amongst them and it would be hard for him to replace them. Our two sheds had been ransacked and Dad's garden wrecked. Dad was furious but never said much in front of Mum as he knew just what she would say.

THE NEW HUTS

When the letter came for us to go hop picking this year, Mum put her foot down. "I'm not going Charlie," she said. "If we have got to go with Horace and Ivy, I'm not going, so that's that. I'm not going to be showed up like last year."

"The trouble with you, Mima, is you worry too much about other people," he said. "I'll get Albert Keary to take us; he'll take us if I ask im."

Mum was much happier now that Dad had arranged for us to go by lorry. People still watched us leave, but Mum didn't seem to mind as much. Other people went on holiday with just a suitcase but we took a lot more than that. We had our bedding and cooking things to take we even took furniture with us. Dad had brought Mum a Primus stove now so as she would not have to cook out in the open. Anything was better than her constant moaning.

79

As we arrived this year, we saw at once that there was a drastic change. The tin huts on the side by the barn had gone and, in their place, stood four rows of white huts. Well, to be precise, two rows of them back to back, and at the end of the first row there were two cookhouses, back to back.

Tom Durman came over to Dad. "Hello, Charlie," he said. "I see you got ere then."

Dad laughed. "What's all this then, Tom?" he asked. "The old places don't look the same."

Tom grinned. "You got new huts, Charlie," he said "Follow me and I'll show you what hut's yours." Tom took out a large red book. "You're in hut number one, Charlie," he said, "and yer brothers, Horace and Albert, are in the rest this side. I'd better give yer two huts as yer have a couple of littluns there."

Mum looked at the huts with a dissatisfied look on her face. "I don't think much of them," she said. "They look like cow sheds to me."

Dad said, "Shush, woman, the man'll hear yer."

"I don't care if ee do," she said. "I speak as I find."

The huts stood facing the barn and we had number one. Charlie and I were so excited. The huts had one little window in them and green doors that locked. They were made of breeze blocks, with roofs of corrugated asbestos, and they were about nine by nine in size. Charlie and I ran to the end of them to look at the cookhouse. It was just like a big hut with no door. On the back wall were three fire places with an iron bar set in each wall for the pots to be hung from. "Oh, look at that," said Charlie, "ain't they cushty, one for each of us."

A large stack of wood stood over in the corner and a big pile of flock mattresses was on the floor. There was a stack of army beds and Charlie was having great fun on one; he was trying to bounce on it. "Look, She," he said, "these beds is hard." He continued to jump up and down on its springs.

Tom came into the cookhouse. "Stop stomping the life out of them beds and mattresses, you littluns," he said. "There's one a-piece for each hut." I was busy swinging around and around on one of the two poles supporting the roof, growing more and more dizzy with each turn. "There's one fire place each," he said, "and the carter will fetch wood once a week, so don't burn it all, missus. I'll leave you to sort out the rest, Charlie," he said. "I'll be sorting out the Londoners at the back."

He walked off. "I would have thought they would have a tap in there," said Mum. "What's the good of a cookhouse with no water, and I'm not cooking in here with no door." "

Whatever do ya want, woman," said Dad. "You got new huts and still you ain't satisfied."

Tom returned. "Oh and the governors don't want no nails stuck in the walls, he don't want nails knocked in all over the place."

"Can't I put one in the back of the door to hang me hat on, Tom?" Dad asked.

"No," said Tom. "The governor don't want nails all over the place, I got me orders."

"Orders," said Mum, "and just look at these beds, they're hard as bricks. How're yer supposed to sleep on that?" She poked at the mattress muttering about us not being in the army.

"Oh, Mima," Dad said, "don't start, don't go on so." Charlie and I ran out. They were about to have another row, we knew. They had one each year that we came without fail. We liked the huts and couldn't see why Mum didn't. They looked better than the old tin hut, that's for sure. They had locks on the doors, so what else did she want? We went to see if our cousins had arrived.

Barry had run off as soon as the lorry had stopped. He couldn't wait to see Dennis again. Uncle Horace and Aunt Ivy had the hut next to the boys, who were in hut two. Our Uncle Albert was to get the hut next to the cookhouse, as our Aunt Liza was bad with influenza and that would be the warmest place for her. Their two sons, Albert and Henry, had the huts in between. The huts really were much better than the old ones. They didn't leak when it rained and with the Primus alight it soon warmed up. Charlie and I thought we were going to get a proper mattress this year, but we were wrong. Mum had us go to the barn for straw with Dad. We didn't mind, though, as we liked to sleep on it because it was soft and warm. The barn was right in front of our hut, so Mum could see us all the time and she wouldn't have to worry about what we were doing.

The Londoners had two rows of huts facing each other on two inside rows. All my father's distant relations were at the back. Uncle Bill

Burden and our Aunt Tillie had the hut next to Bill's sister, Annie. She was a really hard woman. Annie could fight like a man and she often did. She had a large family and ruled them with an iron will. The Kearys were next to them and some other people that I didn't know.

The new toilet was in front of Aunt Tillie and Uncle Bill's hut and this meant that we had to pass them to reach it. Oh, how Mum hated it. "I can't even go to the lav in peace," she proclaimed. "How can I walk past all them men and boys to ave a pee?"

Dad laughed and laughed at her. "You silly woman," he said, "who's gonna watch you go t the lavatory?"

"Well they do," she said. "And what's more, Annie's gone and brought a bird with her. It talks and whistles at the women when they go to the lav. It says I know where yer going. It's not funny, Charlie."

Dad doubled up with laughter. "Well, now I've erd it all," he cried. "Fancy letting a bird stop yer going to the lavatory."

The bird was a minor bird and it did tricks. Uncle Bill taught it to swear and make all kinds of sounds. Mum hated it and wouldn't go to the toilet until she was bursting.

The Eastwood boys went to the same school as Charlie so they spent a great deal of time with him wherever possible. They went in the woods nutting with him during the day when they should have been picking. Mum laughed when they gave Charlie the signal; it was rather like a strangled wood pigeon. It seemed he had a sudden urge to go to the toilet whenever he heard the sound. "Go on," she said "I know a wood pigeon when I hear one." Charlie never needed telling twice, he was off.

FREDDY

My Uncle Bill Burden and his wife, Tillie, were at our farm this year. She was Dad's sort of sister. She was a big fat woman with dark hair. She had a large family. She really wasn't Dad's sister, but his niece. Her mother had died when she was just a baby and it was not uncommon for a woman to die in childbirth in them days. Dad's, brother, Joe Ayres, was her Dad and granny brought her up as if she was her own, feeding her on one breast and Dad on the other. People laughed at the two of them and said that she had drunk all Nan's milk because she was so fat. Dad was tall and slim. Not an ounce of fat on him, so Aunt Louie said.

My mother's brother, Freddy, was back again for a few days. The only trouble was he was a very late riser. He just couldn't get up in the mornings. Uncle Fred was the only brother of Mum's that Dad liked. I think it was because he looked like our Mum. We loved him as he brought us sweets when he came and he always laughed and joked about. He got on with just about everyone.

Uncle Bill Devised a plan to get him up in the mornings. "I bet I can get im up, Mima," he said. He began to laugh. "He don't like ferrets, do ee?" He gave Mum a wicked little grin as he went into the hut. He crept in and put a ferret in Fred's bed, then sneaked out again. After wiring up the hut door, he began to bang on it with a stick. He laughed and laughed as he banged it. "Get up, Freddy," he shouted. "Come on get, outta that bed." Uncle Fred went crackers when he saw the ferret in his bed. He ran around the hut in a blind panic when he found that he couldn't open the door. How the pickers laughed. Uncle Fred never overslept again after that.

THE HOP DOG

The next day I was to get my first glimpse of a hop dog. I had heard all about them from my father. Charlie had been over the far side of the garden when he found one. I was picking with my mother when he returned very excited. "Guess what," he shouted. "I've got a hop dog."

"Oh, let me ave it," I asked. "I've never seen a hop dog."

"No, yer can't," shouted Charlie. "It's mine."

"Well let me see it, then," I asked.

"No," he said, "it's mine. Get yer own."

"Oh, make im show me, Mum," I asked. "I ain't ever seen one, Mum."

Charlie clutched the matchbox that held the hop dog close to his chest. He began to run around me laughing. "She don't know what a hop dog is," he shouted, taunting me. "She don't know."

"Oh, let her see it, Charlie," said Mum, "before I take it off yer. Stop teasing her or I'll tell yer dad when he gets back."

"Tell yer dad what?" Dad said, as he came through the rows towards us.

"Charlie's got a hop dog, Dad, and he won't show me," I cried. "Make him show me. I ain't ever seen a hop dog."

Dad gave Mum a knowing glance and smiled. Dad had always said that it was lucky to find a hop dog. What he actually meant was you would be lucky to find one as they were usually killed by the sulphur that was sprayed over the hops to kill off the pests. We didn't know that at the time. "Show her, Charlie," said Dad.

"No, it's mine," said Charlie.

"Show her or I'll take it off yer," shouted Dad.

Charlie held out the matchbox towards me in a begrudging manner. I peeped inside. "Urr, what's that?" I yelled, as I looked at the long fat caterpillar inside the box.

Charlie screamed with laughter. "She don't know what a hop dog is," he said. "She thinks they look like a dog." Oh, how he laughed at me, and Dad was not much better. Mum smirked to herself. I don't know what I thought they would look like but it wasn't a caterpillar, that's for sure.

"Did yer think there was a real little dog in that box?" asked Dad, shaking with laughter. Mum put her hand in her pocket and took out a barley sugar sweet. "Take no notice," she said. "Come over here with me." I felt such a fool as I hadn't expected to see what I had. Charlie raced off through the rows to tell my cousins about it. He couldn't wait to show it off to the others. I could hear them all laughing so I knew he had told them I thought the hop dog was a real dog.

"Why are they called hop dogs then when they don't even look like a dog?" I asked.

"It's the fur on them," my mother replied. "And they have two little points at the top of their head like ears and one at the back like a tail. You look when Charlie gets back," she said, "you'll see what I mean." I was not about to ask my brother if I could have another look at it. I would take Mum's word for it, as I knew he was just itching to laugh at me given half a chance.

HENRY

My cousin, Henry, was in trouble more than once for sneaking off. Uncle Albert was a very hard man on his children, and he expected them to pick all day. He didn't even give them a chance to eat their dinner. Henry picked hops with a lump of bread and jam in his hand.

Uncle Albert came back from the pole pulling to find him missing. "Henry," he shouted, again, "Henry," but there was no reply. Henry had gone nutting in the woods with the boys. "Where's that Henry gone?" he curtly asked Aunt Liza.

"He's gone to the lav, Alb," she said. "The boy's gotta go."

"I'll give im go," he said, as he stripped the leaves and branches from a piece of picked bine. He strode through the rows in search of poor Henry calling out to him as he went. "Just you wait till I get me hands on yer, boy," he called out. "Just you wait."

Henry returned a short time later; he was crying. "I hate you," he said. "I'm gonna run away."

Uncle Albert just beat him again. "You pick them hops or I'll beat yer again," he shouted. "I'll skin yer alive." You could have heard a pin drop, it was that quiet. The rest of us were too frightened to make a sound. "I bought yer here to pick hops, not nuts." yelled Uncle Albert in his deep voice. "The sooner you learn that, the better you'll be."

That night Henry went missing. We children were sent to look for him. Our Aunt Liza lay back on her bed propped up with pillows, her thin little face drawn and pointed, as she hadn't got her false teeth in. "I wonder where he is, Mima," she said to Mum, "It's getting dark and my boy's not back."

Mum told her not to worry. "They'll find him, Liza, you see if they don't," she said.

Aunt Liza pulled her shawl around her thin bony shoulders, her eyes like little hollows in her head. She sat gasping for each breath, her face racked with pain. "I hope they do," she said. "I hope they do."

Later that night, Henry crept across the yard in front of our hut. He was shivering. I don't know whether it was from the cold or from fright.

"Look at that," said Mum. "He must ave bin up in the hay loft all the time. Poor little sod, I bet he was frozen stiff."

Dad laughed. "Ee wont urt," he said. "That old barn is as warm as toast. I've bin up in it a few times myself as a boy. I don't know how he never fell through them rafters, as they are as rotten as a pear up there."

We heard Uncle Albert shout and then Henry cry out once or twice, and then all was quite once more. Looking at Dad, Mum shook her head. "He's hard on that boy," she said. "He shouldn't beat im like that, he's just a boy." Dad said nothing; he never questioned what his brother did with his family.

THE NEW FOREMAN, TOM DURMAN

The new foreman turned out to be a good foreman. Dad said he was. "He's a fair man and that's all that matters to us, we can't ask for more than that," he said. "Thank god, he's fair." The other pickers had got used to having Mr Lane and they found it rather hard at first.

Tom Durman and his wife, Ivy, moved into the Golding's Cottage. They left the wooden shack that they lived in at Thurston's. Tom's wife was a little woman. She would push her children out to the hop fields in a pushchair, except when it rained. When she came you could see her two boys hanging onto each side of the pushchair. She was such a hard worker. She picked hops just like the rest of us. The younger of her two boys, Ray, was often to be seen with my brother, Barry, and Dennis Steelwell. The older one was always by his mother's side. Our Barry was always away with Dennis and Ray, so we hardly ever saw him. Dennis the Menace and Beryl the Peril was what people called them, because they were always into mischief of some sort or other. Barry was as dark as Dennis was fair, the complete opposite of each other. Dad always had to go and collect him at night time because he was in the Steelwell's black hut. Barry didn't want to know about picking hops, he just wanted to play around, that's all he wanted to do nothing else. He liked to wander around wherever he wanted to. Sometimes he would run to Mum and she would cuddle him. "I nearly got a pigeon, Mum," said Barry. "I nearly did."

Mum just laughed. "Go on," she said. "Don't go too far and don't go in that wood, or else your get lost."

"No," he replied as he jumped up, "I'm gonna get a rabbit fer me dinner, I am." He shouted as he swung around the bines in the rows as he scurried off, "I nearly had one, Mum, I nearly did, ya know." Mum smiled as he ran off, calling to Dennis as he went.

"How come ee don't ave ta pick hops and me and Sheila do?" Charlie asked Mum. "How come he gets outta picking when we ave ta

do it? It's not fair. You let I'm do just what ee wants, so why can't I?"
Charlie went on. "Why can't I go in the woods like im? No, he's yer
favourite, that's why," he said.

"He won't pick," said Mum, "so just let im go."

MR BUNCE

During the day a man called Mr Bunce and his daughter came to the hop
garden in a little fish cart, was pulled by a small pony. They sold all sort
of things and I think that they came on the chance that we would buy
things that we had forgotten. They sold food, cigarettes, plasters, all sorts
of things. He was a short fat man with round rosy cheeks, which his
daughter also had. Her name was Whiney. His main supply was fish, but
he sold vegetables and fruit as well. Charlie liked his kippers, but I liked
the big red juicy apples that he sold. When he arrived, he rang his bell.
We children all ran to his cart, pushing and shoving each other in an
attempt to be first served. Charlie got some kippers from him and I got a
big red apple. "Taste that," said Charlie as he dangled the kipper in front
of me. He knew that I couldn't stand them. "You don't know what you're
missing," he said as he crammed it into his mouth. The smell of the fish
made me sick. I could never eat it, not me.

THE WHITE HART

Sundays were my favourite day, as we went to the pub at lunch time. We children sat on the wall at the side of the White Hart pub, singing at the top of our voices. We sang this song;

No more school

No more stick

No more bloody rithmatic

Life was so simple. All we wanted was a packet of crisps and a ginger beer. Our thoughts were on the present time, and not what was going to happen when we returned to our schools back home. A ruler across the knuckles was a sure thing. That and about one hundred lines of 'I must not go hop picking during school term'. I hated going home. I just wanted to stay in the village and pick hops with all my friends and relations for ever. I tried to get my father to stop in Hampshire like some of the others did. They stayed to do potato picking, but he wouldn't. "It's all I can do ter get yer mother to stop for hopping. She won't stop fer tattering, that's for sure," he said to me.

Quite a few people stayed to do potato picking and then they went on to pick fruit. They went around the farms as each crop became ready to harvest. How I envied them. "Potato picking," said Mum when I asked if we could do it. "Whatever next, child. I don't want yer putting ideas in yer father's head. He has enough silly ideas of his own, without you giving them to him. I don't want to stop in this godforsaken place any longer than I av to." She stood mumbling to herself as she washed up our tea things. Dad shook his head at me as if to say I told you so.

After the tea things were put away, we went to the White Hart to meet our friends and cousins. We were going to the Magic Lantern show. It was in the old chapel next to the Cedars Pub. It had a green door with a black knocker on it. Dirty net curtains hung in the windows and there was a noticeboard on the wall at the right of the door. It was very dark inside, and it smelt very old and musty. Rows of wooden benches and chairs filled the hall. Two men showed us slides from bible stories, as they told us to repent as the Day of Judgement was nigh. It frightened me stiff, I can tell you. I was so glad to get out of there.

Picking was coming to a close and we would soon be returning to our homes once more, sure of just one thing, that we would all meet up the following year. Although we got wet when it rained in the hop fields, we still loved it. We ate our soggy sandwiches under a hop basket, wrapped in empty pokes, quite content. We never complained as Mum didn't want us to go in the first place. We nearly always had colds when we got back after hop picking.

MUM'S BRASS BED

After arriving this year, we cleaned our hut and helped to unpack all the things with Mum and Dad. Then Dad and Charlie went out to the barn as Mum scrubbed out the hut in Dettol. Dad had brought a big brass bed with us this year. He got fed up with Mum's constant moaning the last time we came. The army beds had been too hard for Mum, she liked a soft bed. How the pickers laughed when we got it off the lorry. "Quick, Charlie," she said, "get it in the hut; don't make a laughing stock of me."

Dad just laughed at her. "You talk a load of rubbish at times, Mima," he said. Mum was furious with him and she kept on and on about it. I had my army bed and straw mattress. I liked sleeping on straw as it was warm.

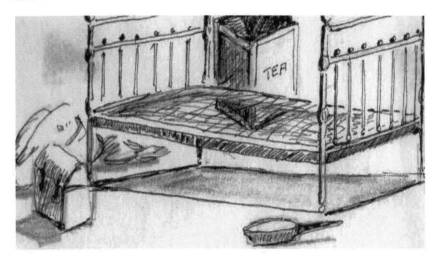

Charlie and Aunt Ivy's son, Sammy, had the hut next to ours and Barry had to sleep at the end of Mum and Dad's bed. She refused to let him sleep in the boys' hut, much to Dad's disgust.

"I don't know why he can't sleep with the boys in their hut," said Dad. "He can't come to harm in the next hut, now can he now."

"No, he's not," said Mum. "He's staying where he is. He's stopping in no hut without heat, it's too cold fer im in there."

Charlie came running into the hut. "Guess what, She," he said. "We got a new tap at the end of the cookhouse."

"Oh great." I replied. "Now we won't get wet when we get Mum water. And we won't av ter get covered in the mud as well."

After getting the hut straight with Mum, I went to the new tap for water. I could see the Steelwells unpacking their few things at the black chicken hut. Our Barry was with them, needless to say. The other pickers were now arriving and children were calling out to one another. "See ya later, see ya in the barn," they called out. Mum and Dad were arguing as usual so I made myself scarce. They always had their yearly row no matter what, and all the pickers laughed at them.

BOYS CLOTHES

I called for my cousin, Vera, and we went to the barn. I could see two boys on the old rope swing. "Who are you?" I asked "Ray," said one of the boys. "And this is my friend, Eddy Croucher." They began to laugh. "What's your name then?" he said.

"Sheila Ayres," I replied. "What's it got to do with you?"

"You look like boys," they said. "Why have ya got boys clothes on?"

"No we ain't, have we?" asked Vera, expecting me to come to the rescue.

"Well, why have you got boys jeans on then?" they said as they ran from the barn laughing.

"You should see your face," said Vera. As she jumped down from a bale of hay she was on, she began to giggle.

I could see why the boys laughed at us as we did have boy's clothes on, because our mothers could not afford anything new. We wore our brothers' cast offs. The boys came back. "What you wearing boys' jeans fer then?" they asked.

"So, you boys can't see our draws," I shouted. "And, besides they ain't boys' jeans, they're girls'."

The boys ran out laughing yet again. I really could see what they meant, though, what with boys' jeans and shirts on and having our hair plaited in a long plait at the back, we could easily be mistaken for boys. Vera and I were rather alike except that her eyes were brown and mine were green. Vera's dad and mine were brothers and our mothers were sisters. It was no wonder we looked alike and were taken for sisters. We left the barn with our heads held down. We didn't want to bump into the boys again. Vera didn't mind, but I did, I was sick of being laughed at. Vera started to laugh; she laughed so much she wet herself. She sat cross-legged at a little low wall in front of our hut, holding herself and laughing and spluttering for all she was worth, making the two dimples she had in her cheeks look deeper than our Barry's. "What's so funny, Vera?" asked Mum. "Why all the laughter? What ave yer bin up to? I hope you haven't bin into any mischief."

"We ain't don't nothing, Mum," I said, "honest." "Stop laughing, Vera," I shouted. "We'll be in trouble if yer don't." But she just wouldn't stop, so I left her sitting there and went into our hut.

Barry lay at the end of Mum's bed. All you could see was his head, his black hair standing on end. He was making sure that Dad didn't make him sleep with the boys in their hut. It was the first time I had seen him eager to get to bed. It was usually a fight to get him in it. "You crafty little sod," said Dad. "You've made sure of a bed tonight, I see." He threw his trilby hat at him. "Don't make out yer asleep, I know yer ain't." Barry gave Dad a cheeky grin in triumph.

This year Dad was not going to be with us all the time. Ashcroft's. the firm he now worked for. said that he could only take two weeks' holiday and one week's sick leave. Dad was to take us down to Hampshire and then return home to Aunt Rose's house, so she could cook for him. Mum felt sure that he would now not go hop picking and that he had to work or lose his job, but as usual he had found a way around it. He worked a week, then came to Binstead with us. I shall never forget, as Mum was worried sick at being left on her own, although she had my uncles and aunts for company.

The day Dad came back, Mum was waiting for him by the White Hart. She ran down the road towards him as he came up it. It was just the way they make people meet in films. He swung her around and around. "I'm never gonna leave you and my kids ever again," he said, "job or no job." It was the first time they had ever been apart the whole time they had been married. It made them appreciate each other more, I think. It gave them time to sort out how they really felt about each other. Rose had taken good care of him, he said, but he was used to Mum's cooking; he didn't like other people's food. "I'd die if anything ever happened to yer, Mima," he said. "I'd rather be dead than live without you and my children."

Mum laughed. "There, Ayres," she said. "Yer soon missed us, didn't yer."

The other pickers laughed to see them; so did my aunts and uncles as they arrived at the huts. "You've only bin away for a week, not a year," said Uncle Albert. "Any one a think yer bin gone fer a year the way yer carrying on."

Dad laughed. "Leave off, Alb," he said. "I missed my Mima, no good me saying I never ,cos I did."

Uncle Albert shook his head and walked away as Dad put his arms around Mum and gave her a hug.

VICIOUS DOGS

I complained to my father that he never took me out when he went somewhere with my brother, Charlie. This particular day, he was going to Hay Place Farm with Uncle Albert. "Oh, let me come," I begged. "You always take Charlie with you and not me."

"All right," he said, "but don't get in the way and no running off." I went with my father feeling very happy with myself for getting him to agree to take me. Dad and Uncle Albert were going to see Mr Durman at the Golding's. Off we went down the dip at the side of the huts, past the forge and down the winding lane that passed the farm workers' cottages. Mr Durman was not home, so they went to the farm for him.

Charlie stayed outside the farm and watched the men at work in the hop kiln. He was watching the picked off hops going into the kiln on the conveyor belt. One man unloaded the pokes off the back of the cart as another stacked them onto the loading bay. The hops then went up the belt and into the kiln.

Uncle Albert went in the front gate at the farm house, and me and Dad followed. "I can't see anyone, Chat," said Uncle Albert. "We best knock the door and see if Tom's about." Uncle Albert always called Dad Chat, as that was his nickname. All our Dad's brothers and sisters called him that. All of a sudden, two great dogs came tearing around the corner of the farmhouse. Uncle Albert shouted at them to get down in a stern voice. Dad lashed out at them with his trilby hat. I ran for the gate as fast as my legs would carry me, only to find one of the dogs barring my way. I can see its teeth now in my mind. It was snarling at me and slavering at the mouth. I could feel its hot breath on my face. It was bigger than I was. It was a Great Dane. I stood frozen to the spot, unable to move.

"Don't move and they won't bite," screamed my father. "For god's sake, don't move." I couldn't have moved even if I wanted to. A man came around the corner of the house.

"Don't move," he said in a curt, irritated voice, "and they won't bite you. Just stand still." He called off the dogs and said not to come through the gate next time we came. We left without even seeing Tom Durman. I don't think I have ever known such fear as I felt on that day. Charlie thought the whole thing hilarious and he laughed at me all the way home to the huts.

"You should ave seen her, she was frit to death," he said to Mum when we got back. "She was scared stiff." I never asked my dad to take me to the farm ever again after that, as once I had seen the big dogs, I had no wish to repeat the experience. I was to get my own back on Charlie just a few days later.

BINSTEAD'S CHAMPION FIGHTER

Charlie and some of the boys were outside the Cedars Pub, playing on the railings on the following Sunday afternoon, when a gang of boys from the surrounding villages came down the road. They started to laugh at our lot, and call them names. "Oh, look at the gippos," they said.

Charlie yelled out to them and said, "Come over ere and say that, I'll knock yer block off. I'll poger yer into the ground." (Poger means hit.) The boys began to laugh and one of them stepped forward.

"Are you the one that hit my brother the other day?" he asked.

"What of it?" said Charlie. "Who wants ter know?"

"Me," he answered.

"He was my brother. He was my brother, so hit me if you can, like you hit him."

"Go away you little wippersnapper," yelled Charlie, "before I give you what I gave im."

Our lot began to egg Charlie on. "Go on Charlie," they yelled. "Give it to im, poger im into the ground."

The boy took off his cap and, before Charlie had a chance to draw breath, that little chap flew at him, knocking him to the ground before he even took off his jacket. He blacked both of Charlie's eyes and gave him a bloody nose to boot.

Charlie got up screaming, his nose streaming with blood. "I wasn't ready," he said. "He didn't fight fair." The men came out the pub to see what the commotion was about. They stood at the railing laughing. Charlie was still protesting at the top of his voice as the little chap that had just beaten him swaggered away to join his pals.

"Did you see that?" said the men to each other. "That littlun's just gave Charlie a thrashing."

Charlie left to the sound of the men's laughter. He had picked a fight with the champion boxer in the area and he didn't know until it was too late. Back at the huts, Uncle Albert took Charlie to one side and said,

"Always remember, boy, the bigger you are the harder you'll fall."

Charlie was to regret that fight for a long time to come, as the other boys never let him forget it for one moment. They called out to him wherever he went, "Here comes Binstead's champion fighter." I had something to laugh at now as well. I had something to call my brother when he called me names in the future. It was like a red rag to a bull to mention it. It was to be a long time before he would forget that fight, I can tell you.

RAY DURMAN

On Sunday, the boy I had seen when we first arrived stood at our hut door. He coughed nervously as he stood by our door shuffling his feet. "Dad said if'n yer all want fresh bread," he said, blushing, "you'll ave to order it or else ya won't get none. You'll ave ta come to the farm fer it, and tell Mum what bread ya want. You'll ave to tell her the day afor so as she can order it for ee."

"Who are you?" asked Mum.

"Ray Durman," he said, blushing for all he was worth. "Dad sent me to tell all the pickers."

He ran off as fast as he could and I wondered if he recognised me. "What a nice boy," said Mum. "I heard that Tom and Ivy had two boys/ He must be the youngest one." She was pumping the Primus stove, trying to make it burn better. "Oh, this bloody thing won't burn right today," she moaned. "I can't get it going. I don't know what's wrong with it."

"Have you pricked out the holes?" said Dad.

"Yes, yes, you soppy man," she said. "I've done all that."

"Who you calling soppy, you silly old cow," he shouted. "I don't see why yer can't use the cookhouse like all the rest do."

"Well I shan't," she said, "so that's that. I'm not cooking in that smoky old place fer no one. I'm not them, froze to death in that smoke, it makes my eyes sting."

Dad was lost for words. Charlie and I were on the bed, trying to make it bounce for Barry. "Oh, go out and play," moaned Mum. "I can't move with all you lot in this hut, get outside and play." We ran out into the sunshine.

Barry disappeared over the Steelwell's black hut as usual. Bill, the carter, was mucking out the stalls in the stables. The smell was just awful and the yard was buzzing with flies. Charlie called out to him, "Give us a ride, Bill, go on give us a ride."

He told Charlie to go away and to not shout. "You make too much noise," he said. "These old cart horses don't like all that noise."

"I bet you let them Londoners ave a go," yelled Charlie. "Yer, I bet they get a ride on them, I bet they do."

Bill shook his fist at him and told him to go away. "Be off with ee," he said, "afor I tell yer father of thee." Bill said he wouldn't let Charlie on the horses now he was older, as he was too noisy. I still watched from the stable door and he didn't seem to mind, but then I never got that close to his horses, and I think that he knew that I was still very nervous of them.

CHARLIE THE TIGHT ROPE WALKER

The barn was just like a big adventure playground to us children. The bales of hay made a great camp to play in, and the low beams an ideal place to hang a swing from. Charlie called out to me, "Look, She," he said. "I'm a tightrope walker." I looked up at the rafters to see him walking along the narrow beams, his arms stretched out each side of him. He dived head first into a pile of loose hay then quickly climbed another beam and slowly walked along it. Soon there was a line of children all diving down into the hay, one after another they went. It was like diving into water, the feeling was great. We dived and dived until we were out of breath and had to stop.

Bill, the carter, came into the barn to see what all the noise was for. "What you littluns doing in my hay?" he asked. "What's all this mess, the hay's all over the place."

"We ain't done it," shouted Charlie. "We always gets the blame. You don't tell them London kids off, oh no it's just us that gets the blame," said Charlie. "You blame us for everything."

Bill told us all to get out and he said that he would tell Dad that Charlie was being rude to him. He also said he would tell Dad about the mess. We went into the little hut in the yard after Bill left. It stood just by the yard gate and faced the stables and barn. It was used to keep hay in and I think it was used for sick cattle and calving. We closed the door and played at being ghosts, screaming and wailing at the top of our voices.

My Uncle Albert heard us and soon had us out of there, I can tell you. "What's all that noise?" he said sternly as he wrenched open the door. We stopped dead in our tracks; I think we were more afraid of our uncle than Dad. He was the one in Dad's family that they all seemed to listen to. He was more like a grandfather to us than an uncle. Our grandfather had died, you see, when my dad was just a young man. He had only just been married to Mum for a short time when Joe Ayres, my grandfather, died.

We ran past our uncle as fast as we could, falling over each other in our haste to get out. "Yer Aunt Liza can't get a bit of rest with you lot," he shouted. "Don't let me ketch yer in the hut agin or else," he bellowed. We did not need to be told twice. Off we ran, as fast as our legs would carry us across the yard.

Uncle Horace and Dad stood in the cookhouse laughing. "That's got that lot out a bit quick, ain't it," they said to each other. "They don't give our Albert no lip."

CARRIE AND THE TIP-UP CART

I don't know who found the tip-up cart but it looked like fun. The cart had two wheels with pumped up tyres and long lathes made of iron that the harness was attached to. The carter drove it out to the pickers in the fields. During the day it was full of pokes to pick in and the carter refilled it with wood for our fires on the return journey to the yard. It was the only cart on our farm that had pumped up tyres. We found that if we all ran to one end that it would jolt you up in the air. Bang, bang, we went until our legs felt like jelly and we had to stop. What a racket we made, shouting for all we were worth.

My cousin, Carrie, came into the yard. She was with a gang of children from Longman's farm. "Can I have a go?" she asked.

"No," said the boys. "You're too small."

"Oh, let her get on," said the girls. "She's only small."

"I'll tell if yer don't," said Carrie.

The boys reluctantly let her get into the cart. Carrie was small for her age and as light as a feather. Her blonde wispy hair flew up in the air as the cart came crashing down. Carrie was rather slow, so when we all ran to the other end of the cart, she was left behind. She flew up in the air like a rag doll. Out of the cart she flew and, before we had time to stop, the lathes of the cart came down across her arm, breaking it. Oh, how poor Carrie screamed. The men all ran out of the cookhouse to see what the screaming was about. We all ran in different directions like hell as we knew someone would get the blame.

Carrie came to the farm after that with her arm in a sling, and we were told not to get on the cart ever again after that. How the boys moaned. You would have thought poor Carrie broke her arm on purpose, just to hear them moan. All out aunts and uncles were at Longman's now, except Aunt Ivy. I liked to go and visit with my cousins, Vera and Louie. Our Aunt Louie was a firm favourite of ours and we regularly went to visit her as well as out Aunt Carrie. Our granny was so pleased to see us whenever we went. She would say, "Come sit with me, my daughter, come and sit next to yer old granny."

Aunt Louie's husband, Jim Lane, sat making flowers made from wood. He was making them for Christmas. I just could not believe that he could make such beautiful flowers from just a stick of wood. After he made each bloom, he would put it in a sack at his feet. They looked just like the chrysanthemum flower head. Just before Christmas, my aunt would dye them all colours and then she would wire them on to a stick of wood, twisting crepe paper over the wire. They looked real to me, and it never ceased to fascinate me.

We never went hungry on our visits as our aunts made big plum puddings in cloths as well as dried fruit ones. Spotty dick, we called it, and boy was it good. My mother could never make it like them and I told her so. My mum and Aunt Louie got on a lot better now that they were at different farms. Mum always said what a hard worker my aunt was. It was just that they could not see eye to eye over Dad, that's all. Plus, my mother had come from a different background to Louie.

BARRY'S ILLNESS

One night, after helping my mother, she sent me to get my father from the cookhouse. "I think our Barry's ill," she said. "He's all hot and he keeps calling out in his sleep."

Dad came into the hut. "What's wrong, Mima?" he asked. "What's all the fuss? You worry about him too much. It's just a chill, you'll see. Wrap im up, keep im warm and he'll be all right. He won't urt." Reaching out, he put a hand on Barry's head and brushed a hair from his face.

In the morning, Barry was worse. Mum kept by his side all day. "I don't know," she said. "My boy looks worse to me now then he did yesterday. He's worse than he was last night. I think he needs a doctor, Charlie," she said. "I'm sure he does."

Dad sat on the edge of the bed, his weight making it sag and groan, as he placed his hand on my brother's head. "He's hot," he said, and it was the first time I had ever seen my father worried about anything. "I'll ask our Albert to take I'm to the doctors," he said. "Wrap im up, Mima, put im in a blanket, keep im warm. I'll go get Albert. We'll have to go to Bentley with im."

"That's miles away," said Mum.

"What else can we do, woman," my father replied. "We gotta do somethin with the boy, ain't we." Off they went in Uncle Albert's old car, driving as fast as it would go. They returned a short time later with medicine with Barry. Charlie and I were in the cookhouse when they got back.

"What's wrong?" we asked, "What did the doctor say, Dad?"

"He's all right," Dad replied. "It's just a chill, that's all. He'll be better in the morning, you'll see. As soon as he gets the medicine down im, he'll be better."

But in the morning, Barry was worse.

"The medicine should be working by now, Charlie," Mum said. "He's no better now than he was yesterday. He's all hot and sweaty, look at im."

I looked at my brother and he was as red as a beetroot. The perspiration was running down his face and his shirt was sticking to his body. Dad went out. I followed him into the cookhouse. "I don't know Albert," he said. "My boy looks worse to me now than he did yesterday."

"Well, Chat," Albert replied, "if I was you I'd ring up that doctor and make her come out to the child. Women ain't no good at doctoring, not in my book they ain't, give me a man any day."

Dad paced up and down the cookhouse floor, before he went to the Golding's cottage to phone for a doctor. After a time, she came. "What's wrong now ?" she asked impatiently.

"It's the medicine, doctor," my father replied. "It ain't doing no good. My boy looks worse."

After examining Barry, she said that she was sorry to my father and that she would have to go and get him some more medicine. She couldn't get out of our hut quick enough. Her Morris Minor arrived back in no time, it seemed to me. "Give him this," she said, as she handed Mum a bottle of new medicine. "I'll call back later to see how he is, but should he get worse don't call me out, bring him straight to me."

After she had gone Mum sat on the bed crooning to Barry. "There, there, my baby," she said. "It'll be all right." Her eyes filled with tears as she spoke. She sat sponging his little body down with cool water in an effort to reduce his temperature, talking to him all the while she did it.

Charlie and I went outside. We knew that if anything were to happen to out Barry that it would break her heart. Although she loved us all, Barry had been her favourite since the day that he had been born. "I think our Barry's gonna die," said Charlie in a hushed voice.

"No, he ain't," I cried. But in my mind, I still had my doubts. I ran to the cookhouse.

Aunt Liza was sat talking to Uncle Albert. "I think that boy of Chat's is done for," he said.

"Shush," she replied as she saw me enter. I sat on one of the army beds next to her and began to cry.

"Is our Barry gonna die?" I asked.

"No, girl" she said.

I turned to my Uncle Albert. "He'll be all right," he said, putting his rough hand on my head. "The doctor's bin and give im some new medicine, ain't she now." It was the first time that I had ever seen this side of his nature before, as he never showed much of his feelings to anyone. I thought to myself that if my uncle said he would get better then he would, no matter what Charlie thought.

"I don't know why my boy got such a fever," said Dad.

"No," said Mum. "He's never ill, I reckon that doctor give im the wrong medicine," said Dad. My brother, Barry, was allergic to Penicillin and at the time we didn't know it, as it was a fairly new drug, and some people can't take it. My family and I would find this out in the years to come.

The doctor came back a few days later to see him. Barry was much better now and Mum was finding it hard to keep him in bed. "Has the child eaten any berries or drunk water other than from the tap?" she asked.

"No," mum replied, "not that I've seen." The doctor was looking at the elderberry bush that grew at the side of our hut. "He's not eaten any of them," said Mum. "He knows better than to do that, and I'm not dirty, doctor, I put Dettol down the drain. I'm always scrubbing out this hut in Dettol, ain't I, Tom," she asked, as Tom Durman appeared in our hut doorway.

"Yes," said Tom Durman. "I can vouch fer that. Mrs Ayres is always putting it down the drains, doctor."

After the doctor left Tom laughed as Barry ran off. "He's no hop picker, missus, and that's fer sure. Ee don't want no truck with no hops, and that's it." Putting his cap on his head he walked away still laughing about Barry.

THE STORM

This year we had very bad storms before we went hop picking. It had rained and rained for weeks on end before our arrival. We children were banned from picking, much to our delight. The poles in the hop gardens had fallen down and were considered to be a danger to us children. The owner said that no child under the age of fourteen was to pick and his farm workers were sent out into the fields to clear a pathway for the pickers to pick hops. This was rather a bind for our parents, but we made the most out of the situation. We played all day, happy as larks, come rain or shine. We had all the baked apples and potatoes we wanted, as well as being able to play all day in the barn. Some of the pickers complained and Dad said they must be barmy. "Them hops is just begging to be picked," he said. "I don't know, Albert, I don't know what's wrong with people, as they're the biggest hops I ever did see. We don't even ave to pull a bine," he continued, shaking his head he walked away.

The pickers were expected to pick whether it rained or not. That was fine if it was just a shower. But if it rained too hard, we had to call it a day and return to the huts. Our Aunt Ivy was the one, though, because no matter how hard it rained, she wanted to pick. She was in trouble more than once because of it, as it made it bad for the rest of the pickers when she did it.

One particular day, Aunt Ivy donned her wellingtons and Uncle Horace's rain mac over her coat and, with a plastic hood over her hat, she went to the cookhouse. Uncle Albert took one look at her and said, "Where the hell do ya think ya going woman?"

"I'm going to work," she said. "I gotta earn a few shillings ain't I."

Uncle Albert had a face like thunder. "Fer Christ's sake, grab a hold of her, Horace," he yelled. "If she goes in, all the rest of us will ave ter go. This rain is here for the rest of the day. Just take a look at that sky," he said, as he looked out across the field in front of the cookhouse. As he spoke, there was a flash of lightening and I could hear the distant rumble of thunder.

"I gotta go to work," she screamed. "I gotta earn meself some money. I can't live on fresh air. Horace spends all me money up at that pub."

My Uncle Horace picked her up by the scruff of her neck and hung her up on a nail on the hut door. All the pickers had put nails in their doors even though Tom had told them that they were not to. Aunt Ivy hung on the hut door screaming her head off at Uncle Horace. "Get me down, Horace, get me down," she yelled. "I'm going to work." How the other pickers laughed at her as they didn't want to pick in the rain and that's why no one wanted to help her down. She was left there until it was too late for her to return to work. What a sight she made, as her wellingtons had fallen off and they stood just below her hanging body. They looked just like two century soldiers on guard duty. "

Oh, get her down," said Mum when she saw her. "Poor old cow, she just wants to earn a bit a cash, that's all."

"That's all," shouted Dad. "Don't be silly, woman, don't be so daft,

Mima, for Christ sake. Let her stop where she is, it'll do her some good, she won't urt." It was some time before she was helped down and even then, she was still ranting and raving at my uncle for stopping her.

Yet another year was at an end and we would be travelling home once more. We said our farewells to each other and began to pack our few belongings. I looked around our little hut for the last time before Dad locked the door, and with a lump in my throat I went to the cookhouse and sat down. My cousins, Vera, Louie, Johnny and Sammy were there. They looked as sad as Charlie and me; none of us wanted to leave as we all loved out holiday. Uncle Albert's two children, Albert and Henry, were there as well. Their older sister, Becky, was with them as she was separated from her husband. She had come to pick hops with her two small boys this year, but we hadn't seen much of them though as they never came out to play. We were all set to leave but couldn't go as Barry was missing.

"I bet I tan im good and proper, when I get my hands on im," said Dad. "You see if I don't. Go and see if he's in that black chicken hut, Charlie, see if he's with that boy of Steelwell. I bet he's with that boy of theirs." Charlie ran to the Steelwell's hut, returning, out of breath dragging Barry behind him.

Barry was kicking Charlie. "Let me go," he shouted, "let me go." He gave Charlie a swift kick to the shins before breaking free and running to the safety of my mother's open arms. With a cheeky grin he turned to Charlie and stuck out his tongue.

Charlie made a fist at him. "I'll get you later," he said. "I'll get you later when Mum's not looking, don't you fret."

We got in the lorry and sat back as it bumped over the cart ruts in the field and out through the farm gate. We knew that we should see it again, it was just a matter of time, that's all. We wouldn't take long to reach our homes now that we had stopped using horse and cart to travel in. That is, all except our Aunt Louie and Uncle Jim.

THE HORSE DRAWN CARRIAGE

Aunt Louie and Uncle Jim had a horse drawn caravan that they travelled in each year when they went hop picking. It was only used once a year to take them on holiday. Other than that, it was stored in their back garden behind their bungalow on Field Common. On our way home we called in at Longman's farm so that Dad could say goodbye to them. But when we arrived, it was just Dad's sister, Carrie, that was ready to leave. "Where's Louie?" asked my father. "I don't see her about."

"She ain't coming," said Carrie. "She ain't got no horse to pull the van. Jim went up the pub last night and got drunk and he's bin and sold it."

Dad laughed at her in disbelief. "Come on, Carrie," he said. "Come off it, where is she?"

"I bin and told yer, ask my Jim if yer don't believe me." Her husband confirmed what she said was true. All the hop pickers at Longman's were leaving; it was just my aunt's caravan that was left out in the field.

"She's bin going mad, Uncle Charlie," said her three sons, Tommy, Mushy, and Johnny. "She's bin and chased father all around this field she has."

Tillie appeared in the hut doorway and said, "Yes she did, Uncle Charlie."

Uncle Albert and Uncle Horace laughed and laughed. "She would," they said. "She'll kill im if she gets her hands on im, that's why he's run off."

"They will ave ta go to Guildford Monday morning," said my father. "There ain't no place round here to buy a horse."

"No," Albert replied. "Jim will ave ta go be train ta get one."

We were told she went home the following week after my Uncle Jim had managed to buy a new horse. It seemed that he had got rather more drunk than usual in the Cedars pub and had sold the horse, unbeknown to my aunt. She was so mad at him because she didn't know about it. She had got all their things packed ready to leave before she had found out what he had done. Her daughter, Tillie, had been sent out to the field to collect Old Bill, their horse, so that her mother could harness him to the van so they could go home. She had to unpack all their things again and stay behind after all the rest went home. his made her very angry leaving her in a distressed state, and the children said that she beat their father with a stick, all around the field when we left. It must have been a funny sight as she was a tall broad woman whilst my uncle was a thin short little man.

ANOTHER ADDITION TO THE FAMILY

September was around again in no time it seemed to me. We were all looking forward to our holiday except my mother. This year we had a new baby sister with us. She had been born in April. Mum was complaining about how much extra work it was going to make for her.

"I want yer to help yer mother more this year," said Dad. "She needs help. So, no going in that barn all the time. You're a big girl now, it's time yer helped out more."

I thought to myself, oh no, why did they ave ta go and ave another baby. Looking out of the hut at the barn, I could see that a crowd of children had gathered in the barn playing in the hay. Some of the village children were peeping over the wall at the side of it. "Coming out?" they called.

"No, I can't," I said in a hushed voice. "I gotta help me mum first, we got a new baby now."

My mother sent me to the tap for water so that she could make the baby a bottle. I asked once more if I could go out and play. "All right," she said, "but no going in that barn."

"Why can't I?" I asked. "All the others are in there."

"Just don't," she replied. "That's all."

I went to the cookhouse and asked Dad why I wasn't allowed in the barn, but he just said, "Ask your mother, she's the boss."

"But she won't tell me, Dad," I cried. "She just said stay out of there that's all."

"Oh, don't ask silly questions," he said. "Just do as you're told for once."

He walked out and so I turned my attention to my Aunt Liza who was sitting by the fire drinking tea and having a smoke. "Why won't Mum let me go in the barn this year?" I asked her.

My aunt looked up. "You are getting a big girl now," she said, "ain't yer. Just stay out of there, my love." Getting up, she went out and went into her hut as it was next to the cookhouse.

I couldn't understand all the mystery of what was going on. My Aunt Liza's daughter, Becky, was sitting in the corner of the cookhouse on one of the old army beds, peeling potatoes into a dish. Looking up at me she spoke. "You can't go in the barn because of Arthur," she said in a hushed voice. "He's bin in a bad boy's home and they've bin and let im out," she said.

"What's he bin in a home for?" I asked. "What's he done?"

"I don't know," she replied. "Just stay away from him, that's all." Getting up, she went out and joined her mother in their hut.

Soon the cookhouse was full of children. "We can't go in the barn?" they complained.

"No one's allowed," said Vera.

Louie shouted, "Me mum said we ave ta stay away. We gotta keep away from Arthur."

"Who's Arthur?" I asked.

"Him," shouted Louie as she pointed in the direction of a strange boy that was crossing the yard. "Dinlo Arthur," she shouted at the top of her voice. We began to laugh. "It is," she said. "Me mum told me so when we got ere."

He put a block on us going into the barn this year as our parents feared for our safety. I don't think that he had done anything wrong, he was just a bit slow, that's all. How lonely that poor boy must have been, as we children were not allowed to speak to him or get anywhere near him.

As I walked back to our hut, I saw Tom Durman at the door. "Well, well," he said, "and where did that one come from, Charlie?" He was looking at my baby sister, and Dad laughed. "It must ave bin that old brass bed, Charlie," he said in his strong country accent. Mum blushed. "I see yer still got lead in the old pencil then," he laughed. As I approached, he turned and said, "Hello, Sheila, my Ray'll be glad you're back, I'll be bound." He turned to my father once more. You timed that one well, Charlie," he said. "Just about right, I'd say."

My sister, Coral, was five months old and was due to be christened in the little village church of Binstead. How pretty she looked on the day of the christening, as one of the Londoners had sent home for a christening gown for her to wear. We didn't have one. Mum was as pleased as punch when Mrs Thresher loaned us theirs. The christening gown had a cape that went with it, which was delicately embroidered with silk flowers all down the front edge to match the gown.

"That's put your nose outta joint now, old lady" said Charlie. "You're not the only gel now, are ya?"

"Oh, shut up," I shouted. "I don't care." Why is it people come out with such silly things like that, I thought to myself, as I loved the baby and I didn't care about not being the only girl. This year was going to be very hard on Mum as she had been through such a hard time giving birth to Coral and her pregnancy had not been good. She really wasn't up to hop picking at all. She hoped yet again that Dad would stop at home this year, but he wouldn't. I overheard Mum talking to Mrs Thresher about it, as it was such hard work, what with the baby to feed and the nappies to wash and the homeward journey at the end of a day's picking. It was hard, as it was all we could do to push the pram through the cart ruts.

When it rained the pram sank axle deep in the mud. What with Charlie and I pulling and Mum pushing, it was no wonder that she was so tired at the end of it all. Barry was no help at all. We only saw him when he was hungry or when it was bedtime. It seemed that he was not part of our family as he was never with us. He lived in a world all of his own that only included my mother. He certainly didn't need Dad, Charlie or me, for that matter. My father complained about it all the time to my mum but it made no difference, as Barry was still her favourite, even though she had just given birth to another baby. He was still the love of her life, her pride and joy and nothing and no one would ever change it.

Mr and Mrs Thresher were my sister's godparents, as the christening robe was theirs. My parents got on really well with them. My father kept an eye on Mr Thresher's family as he only came down at weekends. He had to return to London to work. The following Sunday, my sister was christened, but before the vicar could christen her, she wet all down the front of his robe. You should have seen Mum's face. We laughed and laughed. Mum got very angry with us for doing it. She gave us one of her ice cold looks that she reserved especially for us when we had done something that we shouldn't have and that she couldn't shout at us for at the time. After the christening we had a tea party out in the field. Mum brought a cake and she made jelly and trifle, we had sandwich biscuits and crisps with lashings of lemonade. What fun it was, as we didn't usually have parties except on Christmas Day, and I remember the VE Day party. Those are the only times we had them that I remember. I remember VE Day because we had a street party with tables all down the street to celebrate the end of the war.

MAJOR MONTGOMERY

Dad and Uncle Horace went out for a walk on the Sunday. They always took a walk in the countryside each year we came hopping. My Uncle Horace had already been to the White Hart pub to see the new people that had taken over, as he was the first picker to go in there each year. "Have you seen the new landlady at the White Hart Charlie?" he asked. He had a wicked little grin on his face. "She's got two of the biggest blockbusters that I ever did see," he chuckled. "Talk about cannon balls." He cupped his hands in front of his chest.

"Horace," shouted Dad in disgust. "You'll get locked up talking like that, what a thing to go and say."

Turning to my mother, Horace said, "Don't let im go in the White Hart, Mima. He'll get bowled over by those blockbusters, you see if he don't." Horace laughed once more; Dad scowled at him as he was not amused.

Mum laughed. "You do come out with some things, Horace," she said. "I never know what yer gonna say next."

"We just see old Monty," said Dad, trying to change the subject, "didn't we, Horace?"

"Monty who?" asked my mother in a puzzled voice.

"Surely you know who Montgomery is," said Dad. "You ain't that silly woman, are ya."

Mum snorted. "How the hell was I supposed to know you meant him," she replied. "I'm not a mind reader, ya know. Where did ya see im, then?" she asked. "You sure it was im?"

"We see im over Bentley way," said Dad. "Me and Horace was walking across a field. We walked smack dab right into him, didn't we, Horace? He stepped right out in front of us, because we were on his land and we didn't know it."

"Did he speak, what did he say? asked Mum.

"He just said good morning," Dad replied. "He didn't seem to mind us trespassing on his land. We could ave bin in a lot of trouble if he liked to be nasty. He's a proper gentleman, he is, and that's a fact."

"Come on, Charlie," shouted Uncle Horace. The pub'll be shut if ya keep gabbing to Mima. Let's go."

"Hold yer horses, Horace," said Dad to Horace. "I'm coming."

My mother called out to them as they left. "Don't go touching them blockbusters, Charlie Ayres, do ya hear me," she shouted. "You keep ya eyes on the beer and not on other women." My father didn't reply.

SELLING THE HORSES

Just before dinner the following Sunday, Mum sent Charlie and me to get Dad. "I bet he's in that White Hart, Liza," she said. "He knows we can't afford it."

My aunt laughed. "Yes," she replied. "He went with my Albert. That's the last you'll see ov them," she continued as we ran past her.

"It had better not be," my mother replied.

I ran around the barn to the farm gate. Climbing over it, I dropped down to the roadway by the field entrance. Charlie was already running up the road in front of me. He had climbed the wall at the barn by the side of the yard. All of a sudden, a man came running down the road towards us. He was holding the reigns of a small horse. As he got closer, he yelled at us to get out of the way. We did so as fast as we could and made our way to the pubs.

A large crowd of strangers stood in the Cedars' patch of grass, that was surrounded by railings, and some stood in the roadway below. They didn't come from Longman's farm. I'm sure they didn't because I hadn't seen them before. Some of the men were placing bets and some were selling their horses. They were betting on who had the best horse and whose could run the quickest.

Men were tossing coins in the air and some were placing bets. They were betting who could drink the most beer in one go.

"What they doing, Charlie?" I asked. "Why are they here?"

"Don't yer know nufin," he shouted. "They are gonna sell the horses, and run races down the road, you crank."

The man that had passed us returned out of breath. He dickered over the price of the horse. He then spat in the palm of his hand.

"Errr, what's he doing that for, Charlie?" I asked. "Why did he spit in his hand?"

Charlie laughed. "You're just a gel and they don't know nuffin," he said. "Go away."

Another man wanted to buy the horse that had just come back from down the road, but he wanted to see if it could be ridden first. I could see some men at the end of the road; they were waiting for the all clear signal before starting the race. Then a thin-faced man threw down his cap and they were off. Down the road they ran, eyes wild, their ears laid back, snorting and tossing their heads as they came to a halt. A man came out of the Cedars pub and called out to them. "You know you ent supposed to race up this road no more. You'll cop it if a car comes up the other way, you will. You'll ave the law after thee and then you'll know it, you see if ya don't."

The men took no notice of him whatsoever. They carried on as though he wasn't there. The little thin-faced man came over to my brother, Charlie, and asked if he could ride. "Of course I can," said Charlie.

"I want to sell this horse, boy" said the man, "but that mush over there wants to see it rid first before he will buy it. You're only small and I'm too big to get on it. Ride up the road and back and ya can ave this," he said holding out a silver threepenny piece in the palm of his hand towards my brother. Charlie didn't need asking twice. He was off as fast as he could go, hanging on to the horse's mane for all he was worth, as it didn't have a saddle or bridle, for that matter. When he got back, the man sold the horse and gave Charlie his money.

I could see my cousins, Vera and Louie, they were playing on the railings outside the Cedars. "Is me dad in there? I asked.

"No," Vera replied, "he's in the White Hart with my dad and Uncle Albert."

Charlie was now walking amongst the men. He was listening to what they had to say and had completely forgotten about Dad. He stood listening to my cousin, Mushy Lane, telling the men about a cock fight that was to take place at Longman's farm that night.

"Come over ere, Sheila," shouted Vera as she hung upside down from the railings outside the Cedars, her face going redder by the minute.

"No, I can't," I replied. "I gotta get me dad fer me mum first." I crossed the road to the White Hart pub. I could see my father talking to the new landlord, Mr Yalden.

"I ain't sin a sight like that since I were a boy," said Dad. "They used to hold a big horse fair here when I was a boy," he said with a sigh.

"Did they," replied the landlord. "I've never heard that before. You must know this village very well to know all that."

Dad laughed. "Yes," he said, "I bin coming to this village since I don't know when."

"Dad, dad," I called. "Mum said to come home, yer dinner's nearly ready."

The man behind my father tapped him on the shoulder. "I think that one of your littluns wants you, Charlie."

Dad come over to me "What do ya want?" he asked. "What is it, a ginger beer or a packet of crisps?" He ruffled my hair.

"Mum said to come home, Dad." He just laughed and went back to the bar. He then returned with a packet of crisps and a brown stone bottle of ginger beer.

"Don't go away," he said. "I shan't be long." I sat on the stone wall at the side of the pub, one leg dangling each side of the wall. How long I sat there, I don't know, but my backside was numb. Sliding down, I walked up the slope at the side of the pub. At the top of the slope was a big cricket green, with a cricket hut on the right-hand side of it. A man was pulling a big roller back and forth over it.

On seeing me, he shouted, "Go on get away with you. I don't want you lot up ere."

As I turned to leave, I came face to face with a girl. She had come out of the side gate of the pub. "Who are you?" she asked in a high-pitched country voice.

"Sheila Ayres," I answered, as she was suddenly dragged backwards through the gate by a boy.

"Mum said not to talk to the pickers, Penny," he shouted. "You know she did."

"Spoil sport scaredy cat," she shouted.

Just then, a woman appeared as if out of nowhere and she told them both to get in. It must be the woman with the big blockbusters, I thought, but for the life of me I couldn't see them. She wasn't holding anything in her arms.

I went back and sat on the wall. A ginger-haired girl was sitting on it. "Who are you?" I asked.

"Anne Nash," she replied. "You a picker?" she asked.

"Yes," I replied, "at Hay Place Farm."

"What's yer name then?" she asked, in a soft lisping country accent.

"Sheila Ayres," I said laughing.

She smiled. "Do you live in the pub?" I asked.

"No, Peter and Penny do," she said. "I live at the other end of the village. I'm going to see my friend, Iris. Do ya wanna come?"

"No, I gotta wait fer me dad, cos his dinner's nearly done, and then I gotta find me brother, Charlie."

"Oh, come on," she shouted. "It don't take long. It's just by the church." She raced off up the road and I followed close on her heels. We passed Longman's hot hop kiln and then turned left at the crossroads by the school. Soon we were standing in front of the church, panting for breath. We then stood facing a row of cottages on the right of the King's Arms pub. Anne knocked on a door and a small boy opened it.

"Iris is out," he said. "She won't be long, though, but Rhoda's in." We were shown into a small room with its ceiling bulging and the walls bowed with age. A big log fire was blazing away behind a black fireguard and a large dish, piled high with apples, sat in the centre of an old table. There were a few odd wooden chairs around it and a tatty rug in front of the fire.

A dark-haired girl came to the top of the stairs and called down. "Who is it?" she asked, lowering her head to see where we were. "Oh, it's you, Anne," she said. "Sit down, grab an apple, Iris won't be long."

"Oh, Anne," I said. "I best be going before Charlie finds out I've bin gone."

She laughed. "Come on, I know a shortcut over the fields." We followed the narrow footpath and climbed over the stile. There were cows in the field and I felt very frightened of them.

"Wait fer me, Anne, "I called, especially when one of them laid down on the path in front of me.

Stopping in her tracks, Anne looked back at me. "What's wrong" she asked.

"They won't bite me, will they?" I asked nervously.

She laughed. "Cows don't bite," she said. "Just walk round them like me, Sheila." I wasn't sure if I should believe her or not, as they had sharp horns on their heads and I had never been this close to a cow before. Coming towards me, she took me by the arm and we ran around them as fast as we could, me hanging onto her for dear life. The pathway came out between some houses just a short distance from the pubs.

All the people were gone, even my cousins, and I could hear Charlie calling me. "Where the hell ave yer bin? I hope yer know Dad's bin looking for yer. You're gonna cop it this time, old gel, just you see if ya don't. Fancy running off and not telling me where ya was going," he said. "Fancy that."

"I bin with Vera and Louie," I lied. "I bin in the Cedars."

"Liar, liar," he yelled. "I just sin em and they said they ain't sin yer. Just you wait till yer get back to the huts. Dad's going mad." He ran off up the road in front of me, determined to get back before I could. My heart sank. What was wrong with Charlie now, I thought? He's not happy unless I'm in some sort of trouble or other just lately. We were always together when we were small and now, he wouldn't take me anywhere unless he was made to. With a sinking feeling inside, I crossed the yard in front of the huts and went inside to face the music.

Dad shouted at me and then my mother had a go as well. "Liza was right," she moaned. "She said that it would be the last time I see ya and she was right. I should have had better sense then to ave sent you two."

I knew my mother wouldn't send us for Dad again in a hurry.

PENNY

Sometime later in the week I went to the little shop by the Cedars for my mother. Mum sent Charlie and I to get some soap to do the washing. Charlie was supposed to go with me, but he was too busy talking to the new children who had moved into the council houses that had been built by the right of the farm gate. They were built in the field against the fence that surrounded the field. They had taken up a large part of it, but it didn't matter as it was big. It went as far as the King's Arms pub and right at the back of the orchard. We often took a shortcut across it to get to church, that is if we hadn't got out best clothes and shoes on. As I came out of the shop, I saw the girl that I had seen briefly at the side gate of the White Hart the day I saw the woman with the big blockbusters. She came running down the slope at the side of the White Hart, sucking an ice lolly.

She stopped just as she reached the road. "Hello," she said when she saw me, in her high-pitched country voice. A boy a little lighter in colouring ran down the slope beside her. "We're twins," she said in her funny voice. "We don't look like twins do we. I'm Penny and that's my twin brother, Peter. Where you from?" she asked.

"Paul's farm at Hay Place," I replied. "I just bin ta get me mum some soap."

She giggled. "You do talk funny," she said.

"So, do you," I replied.

"Where you going now?" she asked as I began to walk back to the huts.

"Home," I replied. She began to walk with me down the road.

Peter began to shout at her. "Get back here, Penny, or I'm telling Mum if ya don't. You know she said not to go with the pickers to the huts." Peter had a mop of light-coloured hair and rosy cheeks. I think his eyes were blue, they looked sort of blue. Penny had mousy coloured hair and hazel eyes with the longest lashes that I ever did see, and was ever so slightly smaller than her brother. They were both dressed in school clothes. She was wearing sandals on her feet but Peter had black lace up shoes.

"Can we come with you?" she asked.

"No," shouted Peter. "You know full well Mum said not to."

He turned back toward the pub and she called out to him, "Oh, come on, Peter, don't be such a spoil sport." She stood twisting an Alice band around her fingers at the side of her head. "We won't be long."

Just then my brother appeared with some of the new kids from the council houses. Ray Durman was with them. I continued to walk towards the huts. Penny followed and Peter tagged along behind her. When we got to the huts, Charlie and the others went into the barn.

I went to our hut and gave Mum her soap. "Who's this?" she asked as Penny followed me in.

"Its little Penny from the White Hart, Mum," I said. "She is a twin. Look, her brother, Peter's in the barn with Charlie and all the rest."

Mum looked out across the yard at the barn. "Yes, I see him," she said. "He ain't like you though, is he, dear?"

Penny laughed. "No, we are not identical twins."

"Can I go out now, Mum?" I asked. "I've bin up the shop fer yer, so can I?"

"Yes, yes," she said, "but no going away. It's gonna be dark soon and I don't want yer walking the roads in the dark."

We went to the cookhouse. It was empty except for my cousins, Vera and Louie. We sat down on one of the army beds. We baked potatoes and apples in the hot ashes of the fire. "Coo, ent it nice in ere," said Penny, as she sat gazing into the embers of the dying fire. "I wish that I lived in a little hut like you. I wish that I could come hopping." She stuck a stick into her hot potato and began to knock off the hot ash.

Louie and I both spoke at the same time. "But you live in a pub. You're so lucky, ya can ave all the lollies ya want and drink all the lemonade yer like fer free. Ya can even eat as many packets of crisps as yer feel like eating."

"So what," she said. "I bet it's not as much fun as all this." We stared at her in amazement as we could not believe that she thought we had it better than her.

After some time, Peter came to look for Penny. "Come on, Penny," he shouted. "We've gotta get back as Mum will be looking for us. It's getting dark and you know she said not to go out after dark."

"No," replied Penny. "I don't want to go yet. Just a bit longer," she pleaded. "It won't hurt for a little longer."

Peter ran down the path towards our hut. "I'm going," he shouted over his shoulder as he ran. "I'm not getting into trouble for you." He made his way over to the wall at the side of the barn, jumped up on top and slid down into the roadway below.

Penny got up. "Peter, Peter," she yelled. "Wait fer me, I don't want to go home on my own in the dark." she raced after him calling as she ran.

This would be the first of many happy hours that we would all spend together. Penny gave us free ice-lollies at the back door of the pub when Peter was not around to tell his mother about her. This was not the reason we all liked her, though. It was the fact that she was so daring. She did things that we would never dream of doing. She had some guts, I can tell you. She simply would not believe me and Charlie were not twins. "I bet you are," she said. "He's the same size as you and he's just like you, he must be your twin."

"I ain't," yelled Charlie. "I'm eighteen months older than her." Charlie got very angry with her and he called her all sorts of names. She took no notice of him whatsoever. "Go home goofy teef," he said. "Get back to the pub, buck teef."

Penny took no notice of him at all and let his words go over her head. The other boys began to laugh at Charlie; they teased him rotten about her. "Look, Charlie," they said, "here's ya gel friend."

"If she keeps followin me I'm gonna give her a clout." Charlie threw stones at her but it made no difference, she just wolf whistled at him which made him all the madder.

Penny was a real tom boy. She was into everything. We had a rope swing in the barn that hung from a centre beam. She would swing from it to the other beams just like the boys did. We girls thought her such fun.

One particular night, Penny didn't come to the huts, so we went in search for her. If she was not at Longman's Farm with our cousins she would be at home at the pub, as it meant she had been kept in as a punishment. I remember seeing her hang out from her bedroom window at the front end of the pub. She was dangling a large bear out of it. I could hear her brother shouting at her to get it in, and to not hang out of the window. She did it all the more just to taunt him. She must have been a constant worry to her mother as she saw no danger in anything at all except the dark.

Penny came to the huts one night wearing a fancy-dress costume made of paper. It was a crinoline (a dress that puffed out to the floor). She began to spin around and around in front of the fire in the cookhouse. That is, until my Uncle Albert came in. He bellowed out loud at her when he saw what she was doing. "Get away from that fire, girl," he shouted. "If a spark lands on yer frock it'll go up like a torch. Get back from that fire and get some proper clothes on."

Penny ran from the cookhouse and we followed her to the White Hart. It was just our hard luck that her mother came out of the pub side door for more beer as we arrived. We ran smack bang into her. "Get that dress off at once," she shouted at Penny. "You'll freeze to death in that, what do you think you are doing child, and as for you lot you can all get out."

"I don't like that old cow," said Louie as we all stumbled out the gate. We were all too young to understand that her mother was only doing what she felt was best for her.

All too soon our weeks of hop picking were over and it was time to go home once more. Packing our things, we said our goodbyes. I looked around our little hut with a lump in my throat. Ray stood at the hut door. He had come to see us off before he went to school. "You off then," he asked. "I gotta go," he said. He looked as though he wanted to say more but had changed his mind. Running around the side of our hut, he slid down the dip and called out, "See ya next year," as I watched him get on the school bus until he travelled out of sight.

THE START OF ANOTHER YEAR

Once again, we were all set to go on our hop picking holiday, Mum still as miserable as ever about going and us as happy. My mother's brother, Sammy, was to take us this year, and not my Uncle Horace. As we pulled up in the lorry, we could see the other pickers unpacking their few belongings. Uncle Sammy backed the lorry into the yard in front of our hut. Barry was the first to get out and I wished that I could join him. Mum handed me the baby. "Look after her whilst I make yer Uncle Sammy a cuppa tea. You've got plenty of time to play later, Sheila," she said.

"Tea, woman," shouted Dad. "We ain't got time to make tea."

"Oh, shut up, Charlie" she replied. "I gotta give my Sammy a cup of tea before he drives all that way back home." That's it, I thought they're at it again, they just have to row about something or other.

After Sammy left, Mum scrubbed out the hut with Dettol as usual. She hung up a pair of floral curtains at the little window.

"Get me some water for the baby's bottle and yer can go out," she said. "Yer can go off with yer friends." I ran to the tap as fast as I could.

On the way to it I saw my Aunt Ivy by her hut door. Uncle Horace was with her. He stood swaying to and fro, with his hands thrust deep in his pockets. He had had far too much drink on the way here and was as drunk as a skunk. "Horace, are yer just gonna stand there and watch me try and get this in the hut, all on me own?" she asked, as she tried to lift a tall metal trunk. "Are yer gonna help me?" The locker was an ex-American army locker and was full of tinned food, that my aunt had collected in the months before the holiday. Whatever you wanted, my aunt had it and that was the reason it was so heavy. She couldn't possibly lift it on her own. "Horace," she shouted once again.

"Give me half a crown, Ivy," he said. "I just want a pint at the pub."

"No, I ain't," she yelled. "Surely yer don't want more, yer can hardly stand as it is." Taking some coins from her pocket she thrust them into his hand. "Make the most of it," she said. "I've got no more. Oh and I've got the hopping card this year from Tom, so you ain't gonna get all me money this year, No ya ain't."

Taking off his cap, my uncle stood scratching his head, a silly grin on his face. He walked away, leaving Ivy to get the locker into the hut the best way that she could, with the help of her children.

Aunt Liza and Uncle Albert were unpacking in the hut next to theirs. Their son, Henry, was with my brother, Charlie, in the barn as they had been sent to get straw for the beds, but they were nowhere in sight. Their older son, Albert, who they called little Albert, was now in the army and so he didn't come this year. My Aunt Liza had relations named Harris and they had brought their son, Cooker Harris, with them. Henry and Cooker couldn't stand each other at all. They fought all the time. My Uncle Albert was always parting them.

Suddenly Charlie and Henry came running into the cookhouse. "There's only two horses," they shouted. "The carter said that the owner of the farm is getting tractors now."

"Well most of the farms ave got em here about now," said Uncle Horace. "I spect they ave ta move on like all the rest." He stood propped up against the cookhouse wall. As I stood listening, my heart sank, as I did so like the cart horses, even though I was nervous of them. Returning to our hut, I sat on the bed and watched as my mother made up a feed for my baby sister's bottle. Our little hut looked oh so cosy with the pretty floral curtains that Mum had put up. This year she had brought one of her rag rugs that she had made and placed it on the hut floor.

Tom Durman laughed when he saw out hut. "You got more in this little hut then I got in my cottage," he said, shaking his head. People were milling around outside as they wanted to chat and have a cup of tea with each other. There was a lot of tension in the air, though, as they were unhappy about the size of the crop of hops this year. The hops were very small this year for some reason and the pickers felt that they were not going to be able to earn enough for them. "Longman's is getting sixpence a bushel fer their hops," said Uncle Horace. "I bin talking to old Ernie Steelwell and he said the hops are all the same in all the hop gardens. We won't be able to get a lally [profit] from em if the governor don't give us a better price fer em."

"I shouldn't worry about it," said Dad. "I'll go and see Tom and see what the governor says."

Over the next week there was an air of dissatisfaction amongst the pickers, because they had not got a raise and could not earn what they had hoped to. Some of the farm workers were trying to get our lot out on strike, but they wouldn't do it. "We can't go doing that," said my father. "We'll all get sacked if we do. The best thing to do is for us all to go see the governor ourselves, what doya think?" Dad said. "We can't pick hops at this price."

Dad and Uncle Albert went off to see the governor and later that night Dad returned to our hut very angry. "Tom Durman thinks I've bin trying to cause a strike," he said. "I ain't said nothing about no strike, ave I, Mima," he asked.

"Oh, Charlie, do be careful," she said. "We don't want to lose the money we've earnt up to now. If you get the sack we'll lose it all. You 'old yer tongue and keep yer mouth shut, at least until we finish."

A couple of days later Tom sacked two of his farm workers for trying to cause a strike. When Mr Paul, the governor, asked him why he had done so he said, "I can't ave my farm workers out on strike, I can't ave my own workers refusing to pick, because how will it look to our hop pickers? No, I nipped it in the bud before any more of em thought about causing a strike."

We pickers did get a raise, but not as much as they thought we would because it took twice as long to fill a basket as the hops were so small. Charlie and I picked as fast as we could, but we still didn't earn much. Needless to say, Barry didn't pick one hop. He was off as usual and Dad grew ever more angry with him. Barry didn't care. He just stuck out his tongue at Dad and ran off. My sister, Coral, sat in her pram all day long, happy and content. As long as she had her bottle, she was fine.

LOUIE'S GREED

All our days out in the hop garden went by in much the same way. The crunchy sound of hops being picked could be heard and occasionally a bine falling. Sometimes one of the Londoners would start to sing, and then we would all join in.

We were in the hop garden one morning and it was very quiet. All of a sudden, there was a piercing scream. It came from the direction of my Aunt Ivy's row. "Oh, my goodness, whatever is wrong," Mum asked. "Go see what's the matter, Charlie." Dad stopped picking and went to investigate.

Soon he came back laughing. "I never see anything like it," he said. "Our Horace's Louie has swallowed a wasp."

"A wasp," said Mum in disbelief. "How on earth did she manage that?"

"She was pinching another lump of bread and jam," said Dad. "She thought she'd get another one when Ivy wasn't looking, and a wasp settled on it and she's bin and eat it." He rolled up a picked hop bine and sat down laughing to himself, searching his pockets for a dog end to smoke.

"I can't see what's so funny," said Mum. "The child could choke to death and all you do is laugh at her."

"You ain't seen er," he replied. "Her face is swelled up like a balloon. I ain't seen nothing like it in all me life." Poor Louie, her face was so swollen she looked like nothing on earth. She couldn't swallow as her throat had practically closed.

"That child should go to hospital," said Mum. "She could choke to death."

"She'll be all right," said Dad. "I bet she don't go pinching grub again in a hurry."

Louie never went to the dinner bag again after that, as she had learned her lesson the hard way. Her greed would not get the better of her after what she had been through.

NATURE WALKS WITH UNCLE HORACE

Sunday afternoons were great fun because we children would wait for our Uncle Horace to take us on a nature ramble. He took us into the woods and told us all about the wildlife in it. He knew the names of the trees and what all the wild flowers were called. He also knew where the best nut trees could be found, as he and Dad had found them when they were just youngsters themselves. We children were told what was edible and what was not, our uncle made sure of that. He also went to great trouble to point out poisonous plants, and what water was suitable to drink, such as water that spurted from a bank into a running stream. We all knew what deadly nightshade was as he made extra sure of that, because our Uncle Albert had a little girl called Amy, or so we were told. He said she had eaten deadly nightshade and died as a result of it. She was only small when it happened. "You don't want to die like little Amy, do ya," he would say.

After picking all the nuts we wanted, we made our way home past the orchard. We made our way round to the back of it. "Now listen here," said Uncle Horace. "When ya go in ta get the apples be quick. If a mush comes, I'll give a whistle, so listen out fer it." The boys crept through a hole in the fence whilst we girls stopped outside with our uncle. Soon they returned with their jumpers and pockets stuffed so much they could hardly walk. Then off we all ran as fast as we could. "Don't stop and don't look back," is what he said and so we didn't. He also said we were never to go on our own to the orchard unless it was with him.

When we got back, we made our way to Aunt Ivy's hut where the boys emptied their pockets of bulging fruit onto her bed. After it had been shared out, we went into the cookhouse to eat our ill-gotten gains. Nature lessons in school were never as much fun as the ones that Uncle Horace taught and we didn't forget them. It didn't matter if we couldn't read because we were being taught things at first hand and not through a book.

Mum got very cross at us for going with him. She didn't like us stealing. Dad just laughed at her as he had done it often enough as a boy himself. He saw no wrong in it as long as we didn't get caught. "It's just a few apples, Mima," he said. "That's all, just a few paltry apples."

That wasn't the only thing that got scrumped. Aunt Ivy's children could be seen collecting their tea on their way home from the hop fields at the end of the day. They ran through the potato fields, ducking down in between the rows, filling their pockets with potatoes as fast as they could dig them up. Then my Uncle Horace would bring home a rabbit or wood pigeon for the pot. There were swedes and curly kale growing on other farms next to ours and he would take a detour on his way home and arrive back at the huts with an arm full of vegetables for the pot. They never went without, I can tell you.

"You'll get locked up, Horace," said Dad. "You see if yer don't."

"They gotta catch me first, Charlie," said Uncle Horace. "They gotta catch me first."

GETTING OUR MILK

The fresh milk for the pickers came in tall cans with lids to them, called churns. A woman came to the huts in a little Ford van to deliver it. The van stopped at the side of the huts by the dip and then the woman would ring her bell to let us know she had arrived.

The pickers grabbed anything that could hold milk and rushed to the van with it. I remember scuttling down the dip at the side of our hut with a sixpence held tightly in one hand, in the other a jug for Mum's milk, pushing and shoving like all the rest to be first. The milk was sold to us by the gill, straight from the churn. A gill is a measuring ladle that she carefully lowered into the churn then tipped it into our receptacles. She also sold ice-cream but we never had any as Mum could not afford it. The Londoners had some, though, and our mouths watered for it as we watched them remove the cardboard lids from the tubs of ice-cream. Bending the lids in half, they scooped out the ice-cream and licked at it.

I could almost taste it at times, but I knew it was useless to ask for one as I knew Mum didn't have the money to spend on us children for ice-creams. Mum barely had enough money for milk or food.

GETTING THE BREAD

To get our bread, we had to go to the Golding's cottage at Hay Place farm where Mr and Mrs Durman lived. Mrs Durman ordered our bread in the mornings and we pickers had to collect it after the baker had been. I hated going for it and so did Charlie. He got out of going whenever he could. Mrs Durman was a short woman who always dressed in land army clothes. She wore little round rimmed thick lens glasses and a brown beret on her short, mousy coloured, curly hair. To reach the Goldings' cottage, we took a short cut across the potato field by the black chicken hut. We climbed the stile and walked around the edge of the field. Then we scuttled down the bank in front of the kiln that stood just a short distance from the Goldings' cottage. I walked in to the front gate, passed the fuchsia shrubs that grew out over the pathway, and knocked on the front door.

I could hear a little dog barking and yapping impatiently as she opened the door. I hated this dog as it always tried to bite me. Its name was Bracken and Mrs Durman loved it. She treated it like a baby. It was a small Scotch terrier I think, a snappy nasty little thing.

Mrs Durman peered at me over her glasses. "Yes," she said curtly in her country voice. "I've come fer me Mum's bread," I stammered, holding out a shilling towards her and waiting for my change as the bread cost four pence halfpenny. She peered at me through her thick lenses and I felt sure that she knew that I was part of the reason for her son spending so much time at the huts. I grabbed the money as fast as I could so as to scoot off as quickly as possible away from her stern gaze.

On the way back, I met a girl who lived in the black chicken hut. Her name was June Steelwell. June asked me if I was Barry's sister and I said yes. She then asked me where I had been and I told her. "Can I go with you tomorrow?" she asked. "I can get the bread for Aunty Annie at the same time with you." I told her that I best be going as my mother would be waiting for the bread. As she walked away, she called over her shoulder to me, "See ya tomorrow."

As I drew near to our cookhouse, Charlie ran up to me. "Where the hell ave yer been?" he asked "Dad's going mad, yer gonna get a clout when yer get in. I see ya by the black chicken hut with that girl of Steelwell. I'm telling me father, don't you fret."

"Big mouth," I shouted, "tell im." I stuck out my tongue at him. When I went into our hut, Dad was angry with me. "I want my bread with my bit of grub, not after," he said. "You make sure you're back here in future, I can't wait all night."

The next time I went for the bread, June was all dressed up as if she were going somewhere special. She had a beautiful cream aran knit cardigan that her aunt had made for her. "Coming to the show?" she asked.

"What show?" I replied.

"The show in the church hall," she said. "Me and Dennis are going to go."

"I don't know if I will be allowed to come," I replied. "Me Dad don't like me going to things like that at night time."

"Oh, go on," she said. "Aunty Annie is going to take us so if yer ask yer Dad he might let yer come."

I ran home as fast as I could and asked my mother if I could go. "Ask yer father," she replied. "You know what he's like about you going out after dark."

I quickly changed into some clean clothes, raked a comb through my hair and ran to the cookhouse where my father was talking to my aunts and uncles. "Can I go to the show, Dad?" I asked. "It only costs sixpence, that's all."

"I don't care what it cost," he replied. "Yer not going."

"But, Dad," I cried. "June and Dennis Steelwell are gonna go and all the other kids as well."

"Well you're not," he replied, "so ya can just get yourself back in the hut with yer mother."

Just then June appeared in the cookhouse with Dennis. "You coming?" she asked.

"No, I can't come," I replied. "Me Dad won't let me. Barry and Charlie are going, but I can't."

"They're boys," said Dad. "You're a gel, you ain't going nowhere."

"Oh, let her come, Mr Ayres," said June. "My Aunty Annie will take us and bring us back." She looked at my father with a pleading expression on her face and promised to take good care of me if he let me go.

"All right," he said at last. "But you make sure you're back here in time for bed or else." I grabbed a silver sixpence from his hand and then ran off with all the others across the field in the gathering darkness.

THE CHURCH SHOW

As we arrived at the church, I could see a large crowd of children outside the King's Arms pub. Some were queuing at the side of the Girl Guide and Brownie hut, all shoving and pushing each other to be first in the queue. We went in, paid our entrance fee and sat down and watched as children from the village did their show. The Girl Guides had paper costumes and the little Brownies did their piece as well. We all clapped and cheered after each act.

That is, until a tall girl with long blonde ringlets got on the stage and began to prance about. She began to go through her ballet routine until Barry and Dennis shot at her with their pea shooters. She lost her balance and fell over. You should have heard the boys laugh as she fell. The place was in an uproar because she was a rather big built girl and her top had fallen down. Out popped her blockbusters. She fled off the stage in floods of tears and we got thrown out for laughing, the boys whistling and clapping shouting for more as we ran out into the darkness. When we got outside, Dennis called out to the boys that were running across the field. "Watch out or old Lilly on the gate will get yer."

"Oh, shut up," the boys replied running back toward June's Aunt Annie. "There ain't no such things as ghosts anyway." I noticed they never left June's aunt's side all the way home after that.

We were often to go to shows at the church hall and we went to church on Sunday afternoons to be told bible stories. Penny was always the first in the queue and she mucked about giving wolf whistles to the boys as they arrived. Even so, she never went into the church without making the sign of the cross, no matter how naughty she had been. Anne Nash said she shouldn't do it, as it was a thing that Catholics did, but Penny did it all the same. "I don't want the devil to get me," she said. "You do it or he will." I laughed as she made the sign of the cross once more before going in.

However, she was no sooner inside the church and into mischief as usual. She shot her pea shooter at the men showing the slides to us and ducked down in between the pews. She giggled and messed about like she always did. The men said they would tell her mother if she didn't stop her antics but she just laughed and ran outside. On our way home we ran across the field trying to push each other into cow pats and took turns at throwing stones at the cow pats to see if we could hit them and splatter them.

The next thing was scrumping apples from the little orchard that backed onto the church hall. They were russets, I think, and rather tart to the taste and gave us all the gripes. They were not really ready to eat. The year was almost over and we would soon be returning to our homes, as we did each year at the end of hop picking.

On the last morning, Ray stood at our hut door as usual and said goodbye.

"Goodbye my little Ray of sunshine," Mum said. "See ya next year, my love." Ray blushed; he was extremely shy.

"Bye, Mrs Ayres," he said once more as he walked away. I went over to the wall by the barn and watched as he walked towards the bus stop to catch the school bus. The other children were laughing at him.

"Bin ta see ya girlfriend."

"Shut up," he yelled as he grappled with one of the boys from the council houses.

"Look, look," they shouted as they saw me watching him. "It's yer girlfriend, Ray. There she is, Ray." They pointed toward me as I stood by the wall. I ducked down as fast as I could and stayed there until I could no longer hear their laughter. Then, standing up, I just caught sight of the school bus as it disappeared up the road out of sight.

Why the time went so fast when we went hop picking, I don't know, because the months in between seemed to take forever and ever to me. Reluctantly I helped Mum pack our things with a sinking heart and I didn't care how I did it, as the thought of going home saddened me to the core. It would be the last time that I would see Ray and all my friends for the next year.

AUNT LOUIE'S HOP BINE

My aunt Louie had a hop bine in her back yard. I think it came from Hay Place Farm. As soon as it turned green and hops started to appear on it, I knew that it would soon be time to go hop picking again. I went to my aunt's each Sunday for dinner and tea, along with my cousin, Carrie. All the family gathered each Sunday. Distant relatives just turned up out of the blue. They sat drinking tea in her blue willow pattern cups, the tables laid by her daughters, Tillie and Louie. They used the best willow china. Big plates of cold meats and pickles filled a large wooden table. There was also a large plum cake that Aunt Louie made. We younger children passed the tea around for our aunt and then sat listening to the grown ups talking.

Sometimes my aunt would make tiddly wax flowers as she sat there talking to them. We sat at her feet trying to make them as well. The candle wax was put in a pot on the edge of the fire grate to melt and, when it had, she scraped in coloured chalk from an old tobacco tin from her black apron pocket. The wax was then removed from the heat and left to cool until it was cool enough to handle. A large bundle of wood lay at her feet. She snapped off twigs of it and pruned them to the required shape. A piece of wax the size of a pea was then rolled between her fingers, then pressed between the forefinger and thumb onto the tip of a branch. It was then nipped in at the bottom with the other fingers on your left hand. This made a petal shape. My aunt's gnarled fingers worked so fast that we found it hard to see at times just what she was doing. Stopping, she looked down at us and smiled. "I'll make tiddly wax makers of you yet," she said, ruffling my hair. "Even if you are Mima's gel." There was always that little undercurrent between Mum and her that would never heal. This made no difference in my aunt's attitude towards me. She was always warm and affectionate toward me whenever I went to see her, and I loved her for it.

Mum never stopped me from going each Sunday, although she

moaned at times that it would be nice to have me eat at home for once. "I don't know what you see at your Aunt Louie's each week," she would say. "I wish I knew what the attraction is." It was simply that I loved her company, and the excitement of not knowing who would turn up next with tit bits of news and tales of interest.

I think the only visitor that put her on edge was Uncle Bill Burden. He was a very strange man and so unpredictable. I've seen him on several occasions smash a cup by throwing it at the wall just because it was white. He said he only drank form willow pattern cups. This was not always possible because my aunt always had so many visitors on Sundays. Louie and Tillie made me give him his tea when he came as they were afraid of him. "You give it to him, Shell," they said. "He won't thro it back at yer if he don't like it." I wasn't as so sure, as he was so unpredictable at times.

My Dad's mother, Matilda, would sit out in the garden on a Sunday. If it was a warm sunny day, she would prepare the vegetables for dinner in a white galvanised bucket as there were so many of us staying to eat. Jim Lane, Aunt Louie's husband, prepared logs on his saw mill, the gentle hum of the blade breaking the silence when a log went through, its tone changing as the blade come into contact with a notch in the log. This made a screeching sound, which hurt my ears, but I liked to watch him at work anyway as I was to spend many a happy hour there.

HOP PICKING AGAIN

For weeks and weeks, the following year I packed and unpacked my clothes. Dad laughed. "Won't be long, Shill," he said. "Just a few more days, that's all." I counted them and wished them away. I couldn't get there quick enough. Mum was moaning as usual but then she always did. Dad was used to it so it was just like water off a duck's back to him. Besides, it wouldn't be the same if Mum didn't moan, would it?

Charlie had been working at weekends for my mother's brother, Sammy. He thought that he was quite the little man and he was so bossy towards me. Talk about money bags, he had money all over the place in his room. Uncle Sammy influenced him, all right, as Charlie was more like his son than Mum's. This was due to the time he spent with him. Charlie spent all his weekends and school holidays with him as well. I called him Sammy Cooper and it made him mad. If Uncle Sam told Charlie black was white, Charlie would have believed him. I kept out of his way as much as I could, as Charlie never gave up the chance to get me into trouble.

It was the same old thing on arriving, cleaning out the hut and getting straw and water for my mother before I was allowed to go out. The other pickers were busy unpacking their belongings and having a chat over a cup of tea. Mum and Dad were having their annual row, much too every one's amusement, as it was part and parcel of hop picking to hear them argue. My uncles were used to them and took no notice of it, but the other pickers found it amusing just the same. Fewer hops were grown now, so we didn't pick for as many weeks. We picked for about three weeks in all. There were not as many Londoners either. It was just us lot and a few people from the village.

THE TAP DANCERS

This year in front of the barn, on the right-hand side of it over by the wall, there was a big empty tank. "I don't know," said Dad. "What do they want ta leave an eyesore like that in the yard for. I've never see nothin like it, Alb, ave you?"

"No, Chat," he replied. "I ain't. I think it must be the old water tank at the trough," he said. "Look, there's a new tank, and there are still two horses in the stables. They gotta ave water ain't they."

"Blimey, so it is," Dad replied. "I never noticed till you said. Still, I suppose the horses need it or they wouldn't ave got it, would they."

A group of children were banging on the tank with sticks. Some of the big boys were climbing on it. Uncle Albert shouted at them to stop. They did, thank goodness, as they were making quite a racket. My cousins were standing at the side of our hut talking. "The big girls are gonna do a show," said Vera. "They're gonna dance in the pubs."

"Yes," shouted Louie. "They got top hats and long canes, I see em." Our aunt's daughters went to tap dance lessons and so did some of the Londoners. Our lot started to learn how to dance after some of the London girls danced in the pub last year.

"Are you coming to see them dance?" asked Vera.

"Oh yes," I replied.

"Ya can't see if ya don't pay," she said. "You'll ave ta ask yer mum fer some money first."

I went to our hut and asked our mother if I could go. She said, "Certainly not. Little girls don't go into pubs, you know they don't."

I went back out to my cousins feeling rather resentful. "I can't come," I said. "Me mum said I can't come."

"We can't go either," said Louie. "We ain't allowed."

"Well, let's do our own show," shouted one of the boys. "We can dance on the tank."

"But we ain't got costumes," I said, "and they ave got tap shoes, we ain't ave we now."

"What about these?" said one of the boys from the council houses, as he held up his foot to show us his Blakey's (studs) in the sole of his boot. He tapped his foot on the ground making a tapping sound. "I can get yer some of these and yer can dance on the tank, just like the big girls do when they practice. I've seen em do it."

"We can do our hair in rags," said Vera, "and wear plaid shirts and jeans so that we all look the same, can't we now."

"I got some red silk ribbon in the hut," shouted Louie. "Oh, but you ain't got a plaid shirt," she said, "ave yer?"

"No," I replied, "but Charlie has, ain't he."

Vera laughed. "He'll kill ya if you go in his hut," she said, "you know he will."

We decided to do the show on Saturday when our mothers would be away shopping. We could do each other's hair in rags the night before to make it curly.

That night, we sneaked up the pub to watch the big girls dance. What fun it was. My Aunt Louie's daughters, Tillie and Louie, as well as Elizabeth Eastwood, danced in the Cedars pub. Oh, what a sight they made as they danced in their silk top hats and black silk outfits. They had red silk bows around the waist and red tap shoes. They also had long black canes that they placed on the ground in front of them as they went through their routine. Their heels made a clicking sound as they did so. My Aunt Louie went around with Uncle Jim's cap when they had finished and collected quite a bit of money from the men in the pub. There was also money that people had thrown at them as they danced to collect. They had quite a cap-full at the end of it all. Mind you, they didn't see any of it much to their disappointment, as my aunts kept it.

The week that followed seemed unending to me. I could hardly wait for the weekend to arrive. The show got underway as soon as our mothers had gone to the shops. The girls took it in turn to dance and sing on the tank. This was in front of the children that sat on the wall at the front of the barn. There was a large crowd of children from the village as well. Some were sitting on bales of hay in the barn clapping and shouting for more. Oh, what a din it made and then it was my turn. I finished to the sound of their clapping and shouting just as a group of grown-ups rounded the corner of the huts. My mother was with them.

"What's all the noise?" they asked. "What's all the fuss?" and then it happened, Charlie saw me. I stood frozen to the spot for a moment before making a dash for it.

Charlie began shouting at the top of his voice. "I see ya, old gel, I see ya, just you wait. You got my shirt on, I can see it. I know it's my shirt, get it off or Ill rip it off yer."

I could feel the colour rise in my cheeks as I fled to the sound of the other children's laughter. "She's got boys clothes on," they laughed. "She's wearing boys' clothes." I think I could have curled up and died at that moment, but I ran and locked myself away in the hut. Just you wait, Charlie Ayres, I thought, just you wait.

THE FORGE

I woke one morning to the sound of birds singing and twittering in the elderberry bush that grew at the side of our hut. Dressing, I quickly slipped out of the hut and made my way to the cookhouse, the crisp morning air, making me gasp as it was so cold. Patches of mist still hung under the hedgerows and trees out in the field. Gingerly, I turned on the tap at the side of the cookhouse, sending out a sudden gush of water. Splashing it in my face, I winced at its icy coldness, but felt refreshed and ready to start the day ahead. Taking a toothbrush from my pocket, I hastily cleaned my teeth and went into the cookhouse. I sat down on one of the old army beds and began to rake in the dead ashes from the previous night's fire to see if there was any sign of a spark.

"What are you doing up on a Saturday, girl?" said a voice behind me. "Can't yer sleep? It's a Saturday, not a work day." Turning around I saw that it was my Uncle Albert.

"Oh, you made me jump," I said nervously. "You give me a proper fright." My heart was pounding.

"Yer Aunt Liza's had a bad night," he said. "I'm just gonna make her a drop of tea, gel. Tell yer dad the blacksmith's coming today."

Getting up, I raced back to our hut shouting, "Dad, Dad, the blacksmith's coming. Uncle Albert said he's coming first thing this morning, if yer want ter watch im."

Sleepily Dad raised his head. "What's all the noise for?" he asked. "Can't I ave a lay in without all this carry on."

"But, Dad," I cried, "yer gotta get up or we'll miss im. Can I go and see I'm with yer?" I asked eagerly.

"I ain't up, child and yer asking ta go out," he said. "I ain't heard anything like it. Get out and let me get dressed, or I shan't be going no place. I ain't even had me a drop of tea yet."

Charlie ran into the hut, pulling up his trousers as he stumbled through the door. "I'm coming," he yelled. "Wait fer me. You ain't going," he said. "You're a gel and gels don't go."

"Oh yes I am," I cried, "ain't, I Dad."

"If you two don't stop yer shouting and hollering, no one's going," he said, "and besides I ain't eat yet."

"I'm coming, Dad, ain't I?" I asked, making sure I would not be left behind.

"Yes, yes," he replied. "Now let me dress, child, fer Christ's sake."

I stuck out my tongue at Charlie in triumph. "See, I'm going," I smirked as he gave me a sly dig in the ribs.

The blacksmith's forge was at the top of the lane that went to Hay Place Farm. It was right opposite a patch of rough grass directly facing us, as we scuttled down the dip at the side of the huts. We could hear a clanging sound as my father ushered us over the road. "He's started already," said Dad. "Now I don't want you two shouting and fighting in hear or the man won't let yer watch if yer do. So, no showing me up or you'll feel the back of my hand. You listening, boy?" he asked. Charlie nodded.

Hanging onto my father, we went in. A smell of burning filled the air and the heat was stifling. The blacksmith was a broad man in an open-necked shirt, its sleeves rolled back showing his hairy strong arms. A leather apron was around his middle. He had corduroy trousers on, and on his feet hob nail boots. There was a roaring sound as he pumped the bellows at the side of the fire. Taking a horseshoe, he held it in the flame with a pair of long tongs until it was red hot. He then put it on the anvil and began to hit it with a hammer. Clang, clang, it went, making a ringing sound in my ears. He then put it in a bucket of water to cool and as he did so it made a hissing sound and turned black. He then walked over to a large cart horse, talking to it reassuringly.

"There, there," he said in a soothing voice, putting a big old hand on the animal's back. "It's all right, old boy, I'm not gonna hurt you. You've had this done afor now, so don't play up."

"What's he doing, Dad?" I asked. "Why is he talking to the horse?"

"Shush," said Dad. "You'll get chucked out if yer don't."

The blacksmith put his bottom backwards, towards the horse's front leg and, taking up the horse's front leg between his own legs, he took out a curved-blade knife and began to cut away in a circular motion the inside of the horse's hoof. "Just a bit more to trim off, old feller," he said. He then took out a file and began to file away the excess of the hoof.

"Dad, dad," I shouted. "What's he doing?" not really believing what I was seeing. "Why is he cutting the horse's hoof? Don't it urt?"

Dad laughed, "You silly gel, the horse can't feel it," he said.

The blacksmith grinned at me. "Horses can't feel anything in their feet," he said. "It's just the bit right at the top that hurts, on the inside. They call it the frog." He laughed.

Spinning me round, Charlie began to laugh at me. "She don't know nothing," he said "She's just a gel."

Dad cuffed him around the ear. "Don't keep laughing at her and calling her old gel all the time. You're just a boy yer self, old man."

Charlie glared at me. "Wait till me dad's gone. I'll get yer, you see if I don't. Don't stand too close to that old cart horse, he may think yer head's a hay rick and eat it." He giggled to himself as he gave me yet another crafty dig in the ribs.

The blacksmith reheated the horseshoe and pressed it onto the horse's hoof once more; creating a burning smell that seemed to stick to the back of my throat. It was awful. I watched in amazement. The horse grew more and more fidgety.

"I ain't seen a horse shod fer some time," Dad remarked.

"Well, ya won't be seeing it much longer," said the blacksmith. "There ain't the call fer it now, not like there used to be. Most of the farms ave got tractors, there int enough horses left in this village to make it worth my while coming now. Not now the bloody farmers all want tractors."

"The times are changing and I can't say I like it any more than any other people I know." Dad spoke. "Stinking old tractors, there ain't nothin like a strong old cart horse. Give me a horse any day." Shaking his head, he took us outside into the crisp morning air. Giving a deep sigh, he ushered us back over the road to the huts. This was to be the last time that we were to see a horse shod at the farm forge, because of the introduction of tractors on farms, but at the time we did not realise it.

THE HEDGE PIG

The next night, I sat watching my mother darn our socks in the flickering candle glow. How she was able to darn in such poor light I shall never know. If she wasn't doing darning, she was making one of her rag rugs that she made from strips of our old clothing. Looking up she sighed. "Go on," she said. "Don't sit around me moping, child, fer Christ's sake, go out and play." Out I ran as I didn't need telling twice, that's for sure. I went to the back row of huts to see my cousins, Tillie Burden and her sister, Pearl.

As I rounded the corner of the huts, I could see Tillie. She was standing with a broom in one hand and a baby on her hip. Tillie always had a baby on her hip or in a pram whenever I saw her. This was because my aunt had a big family, and Tillie was expected to help her all the time. Poor Tillie seemed to look after them more than my aunt did. "You coming out" I asked. She shook her head.

"No, she ain't," yelled Uncle Bill. "She is to help her mother, not go flitting about like you do. She's got work to do." I could see her sister, Pearl, so I asked her if she wanted to come out. "No," yelled Uncle Bill, "she's to help like Tillie. Yer aunt Tillie needs some help. She can go out after tea when the tea things get washed up and put away."

My Aunt Tillie never seemed to be doing anything whenever I saw her, not like my mum. She was always drinking tea whenever I saw her. It was Tillie that did everything, not her. My aunt called out to me from inside her hut. "Come in and sit down, Sheila," she said. "They won't be long now." As I entered, she smiled, flashing her pearly white teeth. I think they looked whiter than they were as she was so dark-skinned. Her coal black hair was pinned back from her face, her dark eyes sparkling.

My Uncle Bill sat eating. Looking up at me, he gave a wicked grin. "You get more like yer mother each day," he remarked. "A proper little gypsy girl and no mistake."

"No, I ain't," I yelled. "I ain't a gypsy, so there."

"Oh yes, yer are, girl, born and bred yer are." He began laughing. "You can't get away from what yer are girl. It's no use you trying to hide it, ya can't get away from it. Do ya want a piece of hedge pig?" he asked, holding out a piece of greasy meat towards me.

"What's hedge pig?" I asked, as I had never heard of it before.

"You mean ta tell me ya ain't ever had a taste of hedgehog?" he said rocking with laughter. "We'll soon alter that, my girl."

"Hedgehog," I cried in disgust, feeling sick just to think of it. I could never think of eating it.

He stood up. "Here, try some," he said, holding out a piece of greasy meat towards me. I ran from their hut to the sound of his laughter, as I knew that he would not rest until he had forced me to eat it. I thought that I had dodged him but he lay in wait for me by the back of the huts near the tap. Grabbing me, he forced a piece of cold, greasy meat between my teeth. Pinching my nostrils shut with his fingers, I was forced to open my mouth to breathe. He forced the meat into my mouth. I vomited as soon as it was inside. Turning on the tap I held my mouth under the cold running water until I almost choked.

Uncle Bill roared with laughter as he went into our cookhouse. "You can't say that you ain't a gypsy girl now that you've had a piece of hedgehog. You can't say that ya ain't a gypsy no more, not now." I shook from head to toe and my legs felt like jelly as I went into our cookhouse. Uncle Bill was in there bragging about what he had just done to me.

Trembling, I went in and sat down next to my Aunt Liza. She put her thin bony hand on my shoulder and rubbed my back. "Take no notice of im, my love," she said. "I don't think he's quite right in the head sometimes." Uncle Bill went out, still laughing fit to burst. "Fancy doing a thing like that to the child, Albert," she said, shaking her head. "He can't be right in the head to go and do that to the girl."

Uncle Albert shrugged. "You know Bill, Liza, he don't mean nothin by it, it's just a joke to im. It's just his way, that's all. Keep away from him, gel, and don't go near im if yer got any sense." My Uncle Horace sat laughing as he found it quite funny. I heard him say as I was leaving that he bet that I would not go near Bill again. He was right.

True gypsies eat hedgehogs as they are considered to be a delicacy. They cover them with clay and bake them in the ashes of a fire. When they are cooked and the clay removed, the meat has a texture and taste of chicken, or so I was told. I know that I was force fed with it, but I never got the taste of it as I threw up as soon as it entered my mouth.

Uncle Bill was also known as the unofficial knocker upper. He banged on each pickers' hut door at seven a.m. each day. "Get up," was his call, "before I drag yer out." The pickers didn't need telling twice as they knew Bill of old. My cousin, Henry, was to find this out much to his disgrace.

Uncle Bill knocked on the boy's hut door and Henry didn't hear him. Bill dragged Henry stark naked from the bed in his hut and then locked the door behind him, leaving him shivering in the morning mist. Henry shouted for my brother to throw him some clothes, but Charlie was too frightened to do so. I don't know who came to Henry's rescue but someone threw him some clothes to put on. Henry never overslept again after that. He was too afraid of the consequence and besides, he didn't trust Bill at all now.

THE JESUS MEN

Later that night, a big van entered our field. "Oh God, it's the Jesus men," said Uncle Horace.

"Who are they?" I asked.

"Coma longa me and I'll show yer," he replied. My cousins, Vera and Louie, followed as I walked over to the van.

Two men got out to greet us. "God be with you," they said, smiling. "Is there anyone here that needs our help?" They took out a large white box with a red cross on it. One of the men opened it. I could see bottles of iodine and calamine lotion. There were reels of lint and plasters as well as cotton wool. Soon there were children all around them, shoving and pushing, saying, "I got a cut, mister, I need a plaster."

Uncle Horace laughed. "There's plenty of people to bandage up around this place," he said. "Just look at them."

After the last person was seen to, they put up a white sheet. I noticed that one of the men was unable to stop shaking. I asked him why he did so. He smiled down at me and placed his hand on my head saying, "Do you read the bible child?"

"No," I replied. "I can't read, neither do me brother."

"Never mind," he said. "Trust in the Lord and you won't go far wrong." They told us bible stories and showed us pictures as well. They then took out a magic lantern and showed us slides from it on the side of the van. They kept repeating, "Trust in our Lord and you will never go wrong." The man that could not stop shaking said, "Believe me, He hears our prayers. I am witness to that, because when I raise my arms to our lord in prayer, He hears me. Oh Lord, have mercy on these people," he cried, and as he raised his arms in prayer to the night's starry sky, his shaking ceased. I thought I'd seen a miracle as I couldn't see how he would be able to stop shaking without our Lord's help.

They let me hold their microphone and after what I had just witnessed, I felt privileged and only too happy to do so. They came to us often after that and I loved listening to their stories. Not being able to read it made me all the more determined to do so one day. I don't know what their religion was but they certainly taught us a thing or two I can tell you. We were always pleased to see them.

LOOKING FOR BONES

After attending church in the evening, we often played in the church yard. Hide and seek and looking for bones were often our best games. Charlie took great delight in shining his torch into the broken tombs. "Look, She," he said. "I can see bones." Looking into the tomb as hard as I might, I couldn't see any.

Penny and some of the other girls from the village joined in. We played a game of hide and seek from Charlie. We hid behind the headstones. Suddenly a dark figure appeared at the side of the church. "Look, it's a ghost," said Penny. Because it was so dark, we did not recognise it was the vicar until we ran past him screaming with fright.

"I know you," shouted the vicar. "I know you're from the pub. Just wait until I see your mother, young lady," he called.

"Oh, Penny, he saw you," I cried as we came to the end of the pathway that crossed the field in front of the church. "He knows who you are," I reiterated.

"So," she said. "He can't prove, it can he, and besides, it was too dark for him to get a good look at me anyway."

We would not be playing this game again in a hurry, I can tell you, as I was shaking with fright. The others didn't seem all that concerned about it. "Let's go back," said Penny. "Let's see if he's still there."

"Yes," said Carrie and Vera, and some of the others wanted to go as well. Louie and I were not going back, no matter what, but Penny had more pluck then we did and was all for going back. That was Penny for you, she wasn't afraid of anything.

SATCH

Charlie and I were busy picking hops one afternoon when a small boy came swinging on the wires that ran halfway up along our row of hop bines. He stopped just in front of us. "Got a fag?" he asked. Charlie and I laughed and laughed, as we had never seen anyone like him before. He was wearing a pair of short trousers that were much too big for him and a jacket with its elbows out. Squinting up at us from a large floppy cap, he wiped his nose on his sleeve, leaving a trail across his face in the process. "Gotta fag?" he asked once more in a broad country accent. We laughed so much that Mum came to find out what was going on. I thought she was going to faint when the boy asked her for a cigarette. Me and Charlie wondered just how old he could be. He was smaller than our hop basket. He stood rubbing his right boot up and down on the back of his left leg, before swinging around a bine to face us. It was a wonder he could walk with the boots he was wearing, as they fitted him twice over, I think. His socks hung around his ankles in an untidy heap.

Just then, a woman came through the rows in search of him, a worried expression on her face. "Oh, thank the lord you're here," she said. "I'm sorry if he's bin pestering you, missus," as she dragged him off through the rows of hops. Looking over her shoulder, she said, "If I ent got a fag ter give im, he goes mad."

"You mean to tell me a small boy like that asks you for cigarettes and you let him smoke?" my mother replied in disbelief. The woman nodded. My mother's wondering gaze followed them as they disappeared through the rows to the sound of our laughter. Turning to Charlie, she said, "Don't you get any ideas about smoking, my lad, or you're feel the back of my hand if yer do."

"What's he say his name was, Charlie?" I asked.

"I don't know," he said, "but I'm gonna call im Satch because of his big cap." So Satch it was from that day on. He went around begging for fag ends from the pickers, and hunting the rows for discarded dog ends to smoke. He couldn't have been any older than four, yet he smoked like a trooper.

UNCLE HORACE'S CRISP TIN OVEN

I often went to Longman's Farm to see my cousin, Carrie, as she was the only one of my cousins that I saw during the year between hop picking time apart from Louie. We each thought that the farm we picked at was better than each other's. We bragged about what we thought was the best at each of them. We didn't argue, we just taunted each other in a friendly sort of way. Longman's had wooden huts a little bigger than ours and they had a bunk bed built on the back wall. Some of them had two. Their huts were painted black and looked more like a row of cow sheds than anything else. The only thing that they had better than us as far as I could see was a cookhouse with gas ovens. How Carrie bragged about them, as she knew that my mother was the only one that cooked a roast on Sundays. Carrie's mother did a meat pudding in a cloth and so did the rest of my aunts.

"Well, we can have a roast now," I taunted. "Me mum's just met a woman that lives in the house just by the farm gate, so there."

"Sure, you ave," she said not really believing me.

"Yes, we ave," I cried. "You can come and see if yer don't believe me."

I took her with me the following Sunday.

172

The house we got our meat roasted at was right opposite the field gate. It was at the top of a ridged drive called Thurston's. We found it quite easy to take the meat in Mum's baking tin, but on the way back it was a different story all together. The house was built so high up that it was impossible to come out without running down the ridge drive and into the road below. It was a wonder that we were never run over in the process. Mum sent half a crown with the meat, but the woman didn't want to take it. My mother insisted, so she gave us bags of apples and plums for it, as she knew that my mother wouldn't take the money back. I think that Dad met her first, as he had the knack of striking up a conversation with just about anyone.

My dad's brother, Horace, had his own oven so he didn't need people to roast his meat or bake his pies. Uncle Horace made himself an oven out of a Smith's Crisps tin. Two bricks side by side in the ashes of a hot fire supported it. He made the door out of the lid. He put little wire hinges on it. "There," he said to Mum. "That's what I call an oven, Mima. I don't need to go asking other people to go cook my grub, or pay em fer it."

Mum laughed. "Trust you, Horace," she said. "Only you could think of making an oven from a tin." "A Smiths Crisps tin," said Uncle Horace, laughing at her. His oven never lasted very long as it was made of rather thin tin and there was soon a hole in the bottom of it. "When you go hopping yer ave ter improvise, woman," he said, as he tapped his finger on the side of his head. "You ave ter make the best of things."

PENNY'S WALKING TALKING DOLL

One evening whilst swinging on the railings outside the Cedars, I was to see my first walking talking doll. We were swinging upside down when we saw Penny emerge from the side gate of the White Hart. We didn't take a great deal of notice at first, until we saw what she had in her arms. It was the biggest doll that we had ever seen. None of us had anything like it. All we ever had were rag dolls or peg dollies.

We immediately ran towards, her pushing and shoving each other so as to get a better look at it. You should have seen our faces when it started to talk. We almost took off. It had a string in its back so that when Penny pulled it, it talked. She held it by the hand to make it walk. We couldn't believe our eyes. The doll had long curly hair and big eyes with long lashes. It wore a silk dress with little socks and shoes on its feet. I had never seen anything like it and was truly amazed. We girls took turns to walk it. We pushed and shoved at each other to get at it.

Peter yelled at her to get it in, but she took no notice. He yelled at her once more. "Get it in or I'm telling Mum," he threatened.

Penny stuck out her tongue at him and began to sing, "Tell-tale tit yer tongue will split and all the little puppy dogs will ave a bit." He made a run at her, but she ran back in the pub.

When she came back out, she returned to the huts with us. Peter trailed behind her. He was never very far away from her. I suspect he had been told to keep an eye on her. The big boys were throwing stones when we got back at the huts. They thought it great fun to throw stones at the small black cart shed that was at the side of the dip. The shed was built at the end of the wall a couple of feet from our hut by the elderberry bush. The boys were throwing stones at it and yelling for all they were worth. All of a sudden, a swarm of black bats flew out. You should have heard us scream. We ran in all directions. My hair was very thick and it grew like a bush. On this particular night, I was wearing it lose. I went frantic trying to get the bats out that I thought were in it, but of course it was just my imagination.

Ray tried to tell me that there weren't any bats in my hair, but I was so frightened, I wasn't taking a great deal of notice of him.

Charlie shouted, "Yer got bats in yer air, She. I can see em." He ran off up the side of the dip laughing and giggling to himself. Ray came back after a time. "Take no notice," he said. "There ent none." The other children began to laugh at him. "Durman got a sweetheart," they taunted. "Ray's got a girlfriend." He ran after them shaking his fists and shouting.

As we climbed the dip, I saw to my dismay a large heart on the side of our hut wall. It was initialled RD loves SA. "Who done that?" he demanded. "Come on, who done it?" The others began laughing all the more. Ray was furious. I don't think that I have ever seen him so mad. Although he was a quite shy boy, he had a dreadful temper when roused.

We made our way to the barn where the others were still sniggering and laughing. They sat in a circle in the back of the barn on top of bales of hay. My brother, Barry, and Dennis Steelwell were there, and Sammy and Johnny Ayres, as well as my brother, Charlie and Henry. There were lots of other children too numerous to mention, as well as us girls. They sat smoking their little acorn pipes, blowing smoke rings and telling their stupid jokes. They also bragged about how many hops they could pick and how far they could spit. It was a wonder they never set light to that old barn. Most of them sat in pairs as they were all paired off in one way or other and, although Ray never said anything, the others took it for granted that he was my boyfriend. I liked Ray. He wasn't smutty like the other boys. He never took advantage of the fact that he was the foreman's son. If he had a fight with one of the pickers, he didn't go telling tales about it to his dad. He was well liked by all.

RAY GETS CAUGHT

A few nights later, Ray sat in the cookhouse with the rest of us talking, when we heard his father coming up the side of the dip calling him. "Oh lord," said Ray. "I'm for it now. I ent done me homework."

"Raymond," shouted Tom. We were sitting in the cookhouse at the back, on the Londoners' side, so Ray hadn't got a hope in hell of getting out without being seen by his father. Marching towards the cookhouse, Tom called once more.

"Quick," said Dennis Steelwell. "Hide, get behind the wood." Ray darted behind the wood as quick as he could. We sat talking, trying to look as though we hadn't heard Tom call. Dennis and Barry stood casually in front of the bavins of wood as I sat on an orange box.

"You seen my Raymond?" Tom asked. We looked from one to another.

"No," we answered. "He's not been here tonight, Mr Durman."

Tom Turned toward me. "You sure he's not been here?" he asked. I tried to avoid his gaze as I felt sure he would see I was lying to him. "Tell him to get along home when you see him, Sheila," he said. "I'm going to ave words with that young'un."

He walked away towards the back row of huts still calling for Ray. Quick as a flash, Ray run out of his hiding place and darted around the corner of the cookhouse to our side. "Your father's looking for you, my sunshine," said Mum as he ran past our hut door. Ray nodded and ran across the yard. Climbing the wall, he dropped silently down into the road below. We heard him run for all he was worth, down the lane, then cry out, as Tom had gone back down the dip whilst he was crossing the yard to the wall, and Ray had run smack dab into his father. Tom knew he was at the huts; he didn't need telling where he was as there was no other place he went to. He took his belt to him and we heard it. I felt so sorry for Ray as he must have felt so embarrassed about it.

Ray returned the next day, though, just as if nothing had happened. We pickers were just like a magnet to him. He just couldn't keep away from us. Standing at our hut door leaning against his bike, he asked my mother, "Do ya want anything from the post office, Mrs Ayres? I can get it on my bike fer you."

Mum smiled. "No, my sunshine," she replied. "I've been already, my love. I think yer best get home before yer father comes looking fer ya, like he done last night Ray. I bet yer sore after the belting he gave yer."

.Ray blushed "It doesn't urt now," he said. "But I best be going though."

As he rode off my mother sighed. "Tom does beat im," she said. "I hope he don't run into im on the way back."

Tom didn't mind Ray coming to the huts as long as he did his school work first. Ray was always getting bad reports from school whenever we pickers arrived. Tom received a letter saying how much his work had deteriorated, and besides, the school wanted Ray to go to grammar school. Ray didn't want to go as all his friends attended the school he was now at. He wasn't like his brother, Peter, who hardly ever came to the huts; he kept his distance from us. He was nothing like Ray. He didn't hang about with the boys or talk to the pickers like his brother did. Ray was just like one of us. He wasn't stuck up. I always thought that Peter thought us to be inferior to him. He was the foreman's son and he wasn't about to let us forget about it. The pickers couldn't warm towards him like they did Ray. He had an arrogance about him that said hands off, I'm

178

better than you. I had the feeling that he was the favourite in the family, as he was quite brainy. I could be wrong and I felt that Ray could be somewhat a disappointment for them.

ALBERT

This year Albert was in the army and he would be on leave soon. "Our Albert's coming home on Sunday, Aunt Mima," Henry shouted. "He's coming home."

"Oh, that's good." said Mum. "That'll please yer old mum, I bet."

Becky laughed. "They're be at one another's throats like afor Albert went away," she said. "So I don't know why Henry is so excited."

Mum laughed. "I ain't seen him so happy for a long time." Henry was rushing around telling all the pickers that his Albert was coming home.

The next day I was outside our hut scrubbing the hop stains from my hand in Mum's soapy washing water when I saw a tall figure come out of my Aunt Liza's hut.

I didn't take a great deal of notice at first until Henry rushed past it to our hut shouting. "Aunt Mima, Aunt Mima, Albert's back." Instead of a skinny boy I saw what I can only describe as a handsome young man.

"Is that you, Albert?" I asked. He looked so smart in his grey flannels and navy blazer, its buttons glinting in the sunlight. No, I thought, it ain't Albert, it just can't be.

Albert laughed. "Hello, Shill," he said. "You're getting a big girl now, ain't yer." It was Albert, as soon she called me Shill, I knew. He held out his arms to me and I ran to him. Picking me up by the waist, he swung me around and then gently placed me down.

"You're big now, Albert, ain't yer," I cried trying to catch my breath. He chuckled. Even his voice was different, it was so deep.

"I see yer still the prettiest girl in Hampshire," he teased.

Mum came out of our hut to see what all the commotion was about. She gave Albert a hug. "Come and see the baby," she said. "Come and tell me what you been up to." Albert followed her into our hut and Mum laughed as he ducked down in the doorway. "You got dung in yer boots, boy?" she asked.

"It's the grub, Aunt Mima," he said. "The grub's good in the army, I like it."

"I can see that," she said.

After tea that night, Albert sat in the cookhouse writing. "What yer doing Albert" I asked.

Albert grinned. "Writing a letter to my Eadie."

"Who's Eadie?" I asked.

Albert laughed. "Me girlfriend, of course, who do yer think. Come over here and I'll read it to yer." I don't recall much about it except for the last few lines, they went:

Kisses on paper are not very sweet,
But they will do, darling, until our lips meet.
"There," he said. "What do ya think of that?"

"Albert, you are clever," I said. "I wish I could write and get letters."

"Well yer will one day," he replied. "You're ave a stack of boys queuing to write to yer, and reading's easy once yer start, there ain't nothin to it. I taught me self, yer know. The army give me a bible when I went in and I read it all the time."

Dad walked over to us. "You mean to tell me you read the bible?"

he said sarcastically.

"You can laugh," said Albert. "There's a lot of interesting things in that book they gave me."

I shall never forget my uncle's face when he told Albert to pick hops the next day. Albert said, "No, I'm a man now, you can't make me pick if I don't want to. You can't beat me now for not picking, I'm in the army now."

Mum had a little laugh to herself. "The worm's turned," she said. How poor Henry cried when Albert returned to camp. He was in the barn and refused to come out. Albert's sister, Becky, shouted and called to him to say goodbye but he wouldn't.

"He's gotta go, Hen," she said. "Alb's gotta go. Don't yer want to go ta Bentley to see im off? He'll miss his train."

After Albert left, Henry came out of the barn sobbing as if his heart would break. "Don't go, Alb," he sobbed. "Don't go."

He thought that Albert could stay if he wanted to. He didn't know that Albert would be had up on a charge if he was late back. Henry did miss him so. He tried so hard to live up to his father's expectations of him but it was no good, as he was nothing like Albert in looks or ways. Albert kept chickens for his father and Uncle Albert expected Henry to keep them too, but Henry liked fishing and he didn't want to look after no chickens. As for them taking Cooker Harris on to keep him company, well, it was a waste of time. They couldn't stand each other and they fought morning, noon and night.

PENNY AND THE RABBIT

The time passed by with us hardly noticing our days. They were too full of hard work and our nights filled with play. On one such evening I was outside the Cedars when Penny came out of the White Hart. She began to whistle at Charlie, much to his annoyance. She had the loudest wolf whistle that I had ever heard and Charlie went mad when she did it. "I bet I clout yer," he said. "I bet I knock them buck teef to the back of yer ed if yer keep on. Why can't yer leave me alone."

Penny took no notice of him but did it all the more, just to taunt him. "Yer want to see my rabbit?" she asked. "I'm supposed to feed it after school and I haven't fed it yet." I followed her across the road into the back garden of the pub. As we went into the side gate, Peter poked his head out of the small window by the back door. He asked her what she intended to do. "None of your business," she replied, pointing a finger at her nose. I followed her through to the back garden and watched as she took out her rabbit from its hutch. "So do ya want to take it fer a walk," she asked.

"No, Penny, rabbit's don't go fer walks," I replied. "Yer can't take a rabbit fer a walk."

She laughed. "I am," she said, putting a piece of string around its neck. I couldn't believe my eyes. Peter came running from the pub and dragged it away from her.

"I'm telling Mum about this," he said. "I'm telling of you."

Penny just laughed. "Tell her then, I don't care," she replied. Peter gently put the rabbit back in the hutch and we went to get its food. I followed Penny out of the garden and up towards the cricket hut. Bill the carter's house was by the side of the White Hart and I could see him working in his back garden. Penny suddenly crouched down, motioning me to follow. Putting a finger to her lips she then began to crawl along the ground towards Bill's garden. My heart sank. Oh no, I thought, what she is going to do. I knew she was up to no good

"What yer doing?" I asked. "Why yer hiding.?"

Penny put her finger to her lips motioning me to keep quiet. "I'm getting some of Bill's kale," she said. "I feed my rabbit on it." I watched her crawl towards his vegetable patch, my heart pounding. Bill was digging. Penny reached out her hand and snapped off a piece of kale. Bill's head shot up and Penny ducked. Putting a hand across his eyes, he scanned the garden. My heart was racing. I felt it pounding against my chest, and although the kale only made a snapping sound, it sounded like thunder to me. Just then Penny reached out and took another piece. That did it, as Bill saw her as she ducked down with it.

"I see ya, miss," he yelled. "I know you're the one that's been stealing from my garden. Penny jumped up and I followed, Bill still shaking his fist at us. "Just you wait till I see yer mother, miss," he said. "I'll tell her, don't you fret. I know you too, miss," he said. "I know you're Charlie's girl."

Running, we stumbled through the side gate of the pub. Penny was laughing so much she wet herself. I was still shaking; I couldn't see what so funny about it. "What if Bill tells?" I asked. "What will we do?"

Penny shrugged. "He won't tell, he always says that each time he catches me."

"Yes, but he saw me too, don't forget, and he said he would tell me dad."

Penny shrugged. "Don't worry, he won't, he never does," she said. I wasn't as sure as she was and I worried myself sick about it for over a week or more, just in case Bill took it into his head to tell Dad.

Penny came around each night just to get a glimpse of Charlie. Half the time she looked at him all cow-eyed and he couldn't have cared less. She ran up and down the slope at the side of the farm gate shouting. Peter told her to shut up but she wouldn't. "I'm the oldest," she said, "so shut up. I'm two minutes older than you. Mum said I came out first so there."

"You didn't, I did," shouted Peter. "I'm the oldest."

Penny stood wriggling a tooth that had come loose. "No yer not," she replied through her dribbling fingers.

Charlie called out to her. "Come over here, buck teef, I'll knock it out fer yer. Don't fiddle about with it, I'll knock it out." Penny ran off laughing; she took no notice of him at all.

The rest of us children were rolling down the bank at the side of the bus stop. We remained there until the light faded and the darkness fell.

CHARLIE THE SCRUMPER

Uncle Horace took the older boys out on a Saturday afternoon. They were taken to the woods and surrounding fields to be taught how to live off the land. My brother, Charlie, and my cousins went each weekend. The smaller boys stayed back at the huts with the rest of us.

This particular Saturday, Horace never took the boys for one reason or other. Charlie went with a crowd of boys from Longman's, unbeknown to Dad. It was after dinner when Henry Ayres came running into our hut. "Uncle Charlie, Aunt Mima," he shouted. "Yer gotta come with me, the gavers ave got Charlie." [Gavers meaning police.] "Little Charlie's bin caught scrumping and the farmer's bin and sent fer the gavers."

Dad got up. "Where?" he asked. "Where is he?"

Henry fought for breath. "I don't know," he replied. "Yer best come with me and I'll take yer to the man whose orchard it was." We sat stunned as Dad and Henry went out.

Dad and Charlie returned home about tea time. We were still in the hut sitting on the bed talking when they came in. Dad was furious, I could tell. Charlie had been crying. "I bet yer get put away, my boy, if ya don't listen to me," said Dad. "You see if yer don't."

"What happened?" asked Mum. "What's he been up to now?"

"I'll tell yer what he's bin and done," said Dad. "He's bin choring, [meaning to steel] choring apples and the man's gone and caught im red handed at it. I had to go in front of the magistrate so they didn't put him away fer it." Dad slumped down as he sat on a chair. He removed his hat and ran his fingers through his hair as he moved his head from side to side. "The crank went and told the man he was scrumping," he said in disbelief. "He never had the sense to tell the mush that he was just climbing the tree, oh no, he had to go and tell im the truth."

All this time Charlie sat wide eyed looking at Dad. "I ain't a crank," he cried. "I told the man that I'd done it fer a bet. I didn't tell on the others did I? I said that I'd just met em and did it fer a dare."

Mum laughed sarcastically. "I blame your Horace for all this," she said. "It's all his fault. I said no good would come from im taking the boys out teaching them to steal. I said no good would come of it, it's stealing no matter how yer look at it."

Dad gave a deep sigh. "The crank never had the sense to run like the others," he said. "Oh no, he stayed up the tree and let the mush catch im."

"How could I run?" said Charlie. "The mush had a gun and he was gonna shoot me."

Uncle Horace had been standing at the door when Charlie spoke. He almost choked with laughter. "You should a run, boy, like I taught ya," he said. "They wouldn't shoot a small boy like you for a few poultry apples. The next time it happens run like hell and don't stop fer nothin or no one."

Uncle Albert had joined the building crowd of relatives and friends at the door. "The boy won't get the chance to do it again, Horace" said Albert, "not this year at any rate. I reckon we be a finished picking middle a next week."

The other boys laughed at Charlie when he went out. They called him names. "Fancy getting caught," they said.

"Well, at least I never split on the others," shouted Charlie back at them.

Charlie's little escapade was the talk of the huts for some time and my uncles found it most amusing as my dad was so upset about it. "What's up, Charlie?" they taunted Dad. "Ent yer ever bin caught pinching?" knowing full well he had.

"That's different," said Dad.

"Why, cos the boy got caught?" asked Uncle Horace. "That's all that's different." Dad walked away as he was so ashamed that Charlie had been up in front of the magistrate.

Our holiday was almost to an end. We were to go home the following week and it filled me with sadness. My bedroom at home was larger than the hut we all shared, but I would have gladly given it up to have stayed where I was. My friends and I said our farewells on the last night and we promised to see each other the next year. Penny sat in the cookhouse with Ray and all the others until Peter came to get her. "See ya," she called as she ran down the row of huts. "See ya next year."

I watched her until she was out of sight. Soon the others followed. "I best be off, too," said Ray. "See ya in the morning." Waving, he ran down the dip.

Standing shyly by our hut door in the morning he said his goodbyes and left. I watched as he caught the school bus, and then helped Mum finish packing. It would be another year before I would see Ray and our little hut again.

THE NEW SCHOOL

After arriving home this year my mother received a letter from the education authorities. It said that I was to attend a new school. It also stated that I was not to take time off to go hop picking, and that if I did Mum would get prosecuted. "What a cheek," said Dad. "I'll take my kids where I like and won't ask that lot."

"I don't know," said Mum. "I think they mean it this year, Charlie. Sheila's in a new school, we'll ave ta be careful."

"I ain't taking no notice of the likes of them," said Dad. "Who do they think they are, they're my kids and I'll take em where I like."

"I don't know, Chharlie," she went on to say. "What if they come to the op fields like they did years ago. They sent your Louie-s lot to school one year, if ya remember."

"They can't do that," said Dad. "They gotta catch em picking first, for they can do that".

"We can hide in the woods, Mum," I said. "That's what Aunt

Louie's children did the last time they came."

"Trust you to think of that," said Mum. "You don't know A from a bull's foot now. You need yer schooling."

"Are you gonna take me to school, Mum?" I asked.

"No," Mum replied. "Yer a big girl now, so ya can go on yer own. The other children would laugh if I took a big girl like you ta school."

I didn't care, I wanted her to take me as I was feeling very nervous when I knocked on the classroom door. I entered, timidly knocking the door as I did so before closing it. There in front of me was a classroom of strange faces. I couldn't see one face that I knew. The teacher was writing on the blackboard and I couldn't get over how quiet it was. The children began to snigger. I felt dreadful; they all seemed to have a uniform. I stuck out like a sore thumb as I didn't have one. I was wearing my normal clothes. I began to cough. I think it was nerves that started it even though I had a dreadful cold anyway.

"Stop that at once," the teacher screeched. "Are you making fun of me, girl?" I was stunned and couldn't answer as I was that shocked. He was a small man with a thin mouth and little beady eyes. He wore a black cape and on his head was a mortar board hat. He kept licking his chalk and it left a trail of white in the corners of his mouth. "Well," he screeched, "what do you want?"

"Please, sir, I'm in your class," I replied.

The children began to giggle. He span around on his heels to face them. You could have heard a pin drop, it went so quiet.

"And what have we here?" he said, walking around me.

"Please, sir, I'm in your class," I said once more. A look of horror spread over his face.

"Not in those clothes, you're not," he replied. "Where's your uniform girl?"

A boy sitting at the back of the class began jumping up and down in his seat, his hand darting in the air as he did so. "Sir, sir, she's a gypsy girl. She lives at the end of my road." My heart sank as I thought they wouldn't know who I was, but I should have known better. I could hear the distinct sound of someone chewing gum.

"Who's got gum?" the teacher shouted. "Come on, who is it?" All went quiet once more.

"Please, sir, I'm in your class," I said nervously. "I ain't got a uniform. Me mum can't afford it."

"Ain't," he screeched, "ain't, girl, there is no such word as ain't." He poked me with his cane. "Can't you speak proper English or are you daft as well as dirty?" he bellowed.

"I'm not dirty," I yelled. "I had a wash this morning and me mum gave me clean clothes to put on, so there." I had lost my fear of him now and he knew it. The cane he was holding came crashing down on his desk and picking up a blackboard rubber he threw it. At first, I thought it was meant for me, but he had spotted the boy at the back of the class who had been chewing gum. Brian Price was his name. The rubber fetched him a glancing blow to the head, and immediately a crimson line appeared on his forehead.

I wasn't going to like this school. I could tell this teacher was going to see to that. I started to cough once more and no matter how I tried I could not stop. "Stop that at once," he yelled. "I won't have you making fun of me." I looked at him and thought to myself, I bet you wouldn't talk to me like that if my parents were here. "Why is it you're so late returning to school, Ayres?" he asked. "Why is it that you have had a longer holiday than the rest of us?"

"I've been hopping, sir," I replied.

"Hopping," he screeched. "What the hell is that?"

I looked at him in amazement. Surely he must know about hopping, I thought teachers knew everything. "You know," I went on to say, "the hops that they make beer from."

"Well," he said as he perched on the edge of his desk. "We were going to have a history lesson on Oliver Cromwell, but I think we can have one about hop picking as Sheila Ayres has seen fit to make us late."

He began to tap his cane in his hand as he swung his right leg to and fro under the desk. "Put your history books away, class," he said, "and no talking now, as Sheila Ayres is going to take the lesson." I could see that the class was stunned but no more than I was. I could hear their sniggers and see their silly faces as they wriggled in their seats. "Well," he snapped, "I'm waiting."

I stood transfixed. I definitely was not going to like this school. A sudden surge of anger filled me almost to the point of bursting. How dare they laugh at me, I thought, I'll show them. Turning to the teacher, I found myself answering in a calm clear voice. "I don't remember," I said. "We just picked hops that's all."

The teacher's face went purple. He sprang from his perch and leaned towards me, his face almost touching mine. "You dare to cross me, girl," he snapped, daring me to answer him. I could see a nervous little twitch appear in the corner of his eye. "You've just got back and you can't remember how it's done."

"No, I don't remember," I replied once more. It's your turn to feel a fool now I thought. I wonder how you like it.

How could I tell that lot what it was like to go hop picking? I could see they would never understand what it would be like to sleep on hay or drink fresh water from a spring or even eat food that had been cooked on an open fire. No, I wouldn't tell him or them and he couldn't make me.

"Get to the back of the class," he yelled. "Get out of my sight." I don't think he had ever had a child answer him back before and he couldn't handle it. It completely threw him. I don't think I shall ever forget my humiliation that day. I did try hard at school but just couldn't catch up. I couldn't get them to understand that the harder I tried the harder it got. The letters all jumbled into a meaningless mess and my mind went blank. I often wrote back to front and the simplest things just vanished from my mind. I just couldn't retain what I had learned for very long. I would be having a lesson on tea pickers in Ceylon one minute and be hop picking the next. "What did I say, Ayres?" said this particular teacher. "Tell us what's picked in the baskets."

"Hops, miss," I replied. "The basket holds five bushels." The whole class was in an uproar.

"Get out," she screamed. "Get out and see me after school." She thought I was making fun of her. It didn't enter into her head that I wasn't and besides, I hadn't got that one important thing above all else, *a school uniform*, and I never went on one school trip because of it. It did not seem to matter to them that my parents could not afford one and that I had no say in the matter. They penalised me just the same. How I wished I was clever, but I wasn't. I often complained about it to my mother's friend, Margie.

Margie lived next door to us and she had a very large family. I often helped out in her house as her children were all small. She found it hard to cope at times and was only too happy for me to give her a hand with them. "It wouldn't be right if everyone was clever," she said. "God gives us all gifts of some kind or other, so don't feel bad. You are clever at things that people with brains can't do. It wouldn't be right if we were all the same, would it?" I didn't know about that. I would have just been happy to be able to read properly and spell, as well as tell the time. That's all.

SAD NEWS

At the end of April, we received some sad news. My cousins, Vera and Louie Ayres, came to tea on Sunday. This time they brought with them a letter from Binstead. One of the girls from the village had sent it, and she had sent a newspaper cutting with it.

I was upstairs when they arrived. Charlie called me down. "Louie and Vera are here," he said. There was something in the tone of his voice that made me feel uneasy. Mum and Dad were reading the newspaper cutting.

"I don't know," said Mum, shaking her head reverently. "That poor woman must be off er head."

"She ain't ad no luck since she's bin in that pub," said Dad.

"What pub?" I asked. "What's wrong?"

Charlie spoke in nearly a whisper. "It's little Penny, she's, she's bin drowned."

"Don't be silly," I cried. "Who told yer that?"

"Louie," he said. "Look, she's got a letter from Anne Nash and Iris." He held out the letter towards me. I took it with shaking hands.

Louie spoke. "We gotta go, Sheila," she said. "We gotta go and tell Carrie and the others about it. We thought you would want to know first, that's why we came to tell ya."

I felt numb as I went back up to my room. I just could not believe that it was true. I'd hoped it would be a bad dream and that I would wake up in bed at any moment. I read what I could of the letter over and over; I just couldn't accept that she was dead. She just couldn't be. I cried until I couldn't cry any more, as I went over in my mind all the things we had done together. I could picture her face before and hear her high-pitched laugh. I had never lost a person that I was so fond of before, especially one so young. I just could not imagine the White Hart without her in it or Peter without her by his side. It took the joy out of going this year as I just could not bring myself to look forward to it

We packed our things and made our way to Binstead as usual and, on our arrival, we noticed a wire fence all-round the cookhouse. Uncle Sammy laughed. "Well now I've seen it all," he said. "Look, Mima, they bin and fenced yer in so yer can't run off."

"Shut up, Sam," said Dad. "Don't make Mima worse. You know she don't need you to make her start."

Uncle Sammy laughed all the more. "They're frightened you'll pack up and go home," he said, laughing fit to burst. "That's why they put this fence up."

Dad got out of the lorry and cut the wire. "There's cows out there," he said, pointing towards the field. "Look, can't yer see em? That's what this fence is up for."

Mum began to moan. "We're just like animals," she said. "Look at what we gotta live in. Pigs live like this and fer what, just so we can earn a few poultry shillings."

"Now look at what yer bin and done, Sam," said Dad. "She's bad enough without the likes of you setting her off."

We washed out our hut and moved in our things. "Can I go out, Mum?" I asked. "I've done all the unpacking and got yer water."

"Yes, yes," she said, "off yer go." I didn't need telling twice. I was off.

Wandering across the barn I sat down. The barn seemed oh, so empty and I knew it was never going to be the same again. Without Penny's presence how could it be? Hearing a noise, I looked up at Louie and Vera coming in. They sat down. "It ain't gonna be the same this year. It won't be the same without Penny, will it?" they said.

"I still think she's gonna jump off a beam," said Louie.

"So do I," said Vera reverently. "Don't you?"

I nodded. The old rope swing we had all used hung swinging gently to a fro in the breeze. I could almost see Penny swinging on it. I swallowed hard, trying to move a lump in my throat, but it wouldn't shift. Ray Durman and some of the others came in and sat down; they were all talking about Penny. I don't think that anyone could believe that she was dead. Dennis Steelwell took down the old rope swing and it was cut into pieces, and we all had a piece as a keepsake to remember her by.

On Sunday I went to the church yard to find her grave. When I arrived, I saw my cousins as well. "What's wrong? I asked as I saw their faces. "What's up?"

"She ain't here," said Carrie. "We bin and searched this church yard inside out and she ain't in it."

Charlie walked over to us and asked what was wrong. "Of course she's in ere," said Charlie. "She must be."

"No, she ain't," the others said. "You look fer yerself." Charlie and I searched in vain for it but couldn't find it. A man working in the church yard asked us what we were doing. "We ain't doing nuffin," Charlie replied. "We're just searching for little Penny's grave, that's all."

"She ent ere," said the man. "She weren't put ta rest in this church yard. I should know if she were." We ran from the church and slowly made our way back to the huts. As we passed the White Hart I stopped and looked up at the small window that Penny had hung out of so many times in the past. I just could not accept that she would not be there. When I grow up and have children, I vowed, I'm going to call my first daughter Penny so I never forget you. I also vowed to find her grave and put the biggest bunch of flowers upon it. The others were way out in front of me as I ran to catch up. They were still puzzled as to her whereabouts, and they just couldn't understand it.

As we drew near the huts Ray came to meet us. "Where you bin?"

he asked. Climbing the dip, we told him.

"It ain't there," said Louie. "We can't find it."

"Well ya won't," he replied. "She not buried in this village. She's buried out Bordon way, agin her grandfather. I think Peter and his mum are gonna move away. They're gonna leave the pub. I think Charlie Collins, the bar man, is going with em."

My heart sank. I had so looked forward to putting flowers on her grave, and now I had been robbed of even doing that. Mum called out to us to go in for our tea, so we did.

"Where the hell ave yer bin?" asked Dad. "Look at the time."

"We bin searching fer little Penny's grave, Dad" said Charlie. "We couldn't find it."

"What!" shouted Dad. "You keep out a that church yard or you'll get locked up."

"But, Dad, we was just looking fer little Penny's grave, that's all," I cried. "We weren't doing no harm."

"She ain't there, anyway," said Charlie. "She's at Bordon, Ray Durman told us."

"Will you take us to find it, Dad?" I asked. He almost choked on the tea he was drinking.

"That's miles away," he shouted. "No, yer don't want ta go searching fer no graves, child, whatever next. Besides," he went on to say, "I don't know where that poor child's buried."

"You can ask her mum," I said.

"What?" screeched Dad. "How can I ask that poor woman where her child's buried? Don't keep on. You just eat yer grub and forget about it." He shook his head.

How I could forget a thing like that, I thought. He must be joking if he thinks that I would forget a thing like that. I knew that I should never be able to forget Penny. I just knew it, and when I did have my first child, a girl, I called her Penny.

CORAL'S NARROW ESCAPE

"I want yer to take the baby out," said Dad, "to give yer mother a rest. It won't hurt yer to look after her for a while. Take her to see yer granny at Longman's, she don't see much of the baby. Don't go messing about with her, though. You're a big girl now, so look after her properly." A big girl I thought, it's funny how I'm a big girl whenever they expect me to look after the baby, but it's a different thing all together when I ask to go and see the church show, or in fact to do anything I wanted.

I wheeled the pram to the cookhouse. Louie and Vera were sitting by the fire; they were poking around in the ashes for their baked potatoes. "Coming to Longman's?" I asked, as I wheeled the pram towards them. "Me dad said I gotta take the baby to see Granny Ayres."

Coral sat in her pram, grizzling as always. She always cried when I had to look after her. Louie rocked the handle of the pram and she stopped crying and began to smile. "Come on then," said Vera. "It'll be dark soon." We made our way around the barbed wire that surrounded the cookhouse and went out of the farm gate. Louie and Vera pushed and shoved at each other in an attempt to get at my sister. I wasn't supposed to let them have her as she had been left in my care.

I pushed the pram hard and let go, but only for a second, though. As I grabbed the pram back by the handle, it jolted the baby into the air. Louie begged me to let her have a go. "Go on," she said. "Yer dad won't know if yer do."

Vera pushed at her. "I'm having a go," she said. I didn't care who had a go as long as it wasn't me. I was sick of having to look after her.

"You can push her as far as the pub, Louie," I said, "then its Vera's turn till we reach Longman's." They both agreed and we continued our journey.

All went well until we reached Longman's hop kiln. Louie grabbed at the pram handle, giving it a hard push, pushing the pram away from her. Vera screamed. I stood frozen to the spot as she attempted to grab it. Louie covered her eyes as there was a car coming towards the pram. I could see the chrome glinting on the pram wheels as it passed the open kiln door. A crowd of children were sitting on the school steps, and some were sitting in the roots of the old tree by the school, their faces peering out of the roots. It was all over in a matter of seconds, but to me it seemed to take forever. It seemed as though it was in slow motion. The car screeched to a halt and a man got out. He was so angry. Vera raced after the pram as I was still unable to move.

"You stupid girl," yelled the man. "I could have killed that child."

Vera's face was scarlet. "It's not my baby," she said. "It's not my fault, I never done it." The man got back in his car and drove away. Meanwhile the children that were sitting on the steps came across the road shouting at us.

"You stupid girl," they mimicked. "I could have killed that child." Vera told them to shut up and go away. I was just so thankful that my sister had come to no real harm. I would never let them push her ever again after that as I knew that I should be in for a real thrashing if Dad ever found out.

LILLY ON THE GATE

Just a few days after the incident with Coral, a few of us were out in the fields in front of the cookhouse playing tag. We knew that our mothers wanted us to go in, but we pretended not to notice them. I could see my mother by the side of the cookhouse with Aunt Ivy. "Come on in now," she called. She stood wiping her hands on her apron. "It's getting dark now and I want you in," she said.

"A fat chance you got of getin them in," said Uncle Horace. "They can hear ya they just don't want ta."

Mum nodded. "I know," she said. "But it's getting late." It was the night of the full moon, so it was quite light out in the field, and we were having too much fun to go in. Suddenly we were standing in darkness as the moon was covered by cloud. You couldn't see a hand in front of you.

Looking up I saw a thing on the gate over by the Steelwells black chicken hut. All that I could see was a pair of glowing eyes and a stream of light from a gash shaped mouth. I let out a piercing scream, causing the others to look up. Louie was over the far side when I screamed, so she was the last one to see it. We all knew the tale of the ghost that was supposed to sit on the gate and haunt the farm. We had been told about it often enough. I thought it was just something the gown ups had thought up to get us in after dark. They said she sat on the gate when the moon was full. On seeing the thing on the gate, we all took off across the field as fast as we could, stumbling and falling all over the place. Louie ran as if the devil himself was after her, across the field towards the light of the cookhouse, but just as she reached it, she fell splat on her face into a cowpat.

What a mess she was in, with her clothes all covered in cow dung, and it dripped from her face and hands. Aunt Ivy went ma.d "Go on, go and wash it off," she yelled. "You ain't coming in this hut all covered in cow shit."

The men came out of the cookhouse to see what all the commotion was about, and how they laughed when they saw her. "That's got em in, Mima," said Uncle Horace. "Who's idea was that?"

I found out later that night that it was Barry and Dennis. They had done it to frighten us older ones and it worked, I can tell you. They had hollowed out a mangle (vegetable like a swede) and put a lighted candle inside its carved-out face so as to give it a ghostly glow. (The same way you do a pumpkin at Halloween).

"Trust my Louie to find a fresh cowpat," said Uncle Horace. "Trust her." Dad laughed and Mum was finding it rather hard to stop herself from laughing. Louie stood at the tap trying to wash it off, shivering with the cold, her teeth chattering.

BARRY AND DENNIS ON THE HAMPSHIRE WAGON

I never saw much of my brother, Barry, whenever we went hop picking as he was always off some place or other with Dennis Steelwell. I don't even remember him picking one hop. Barry would spend the whole day nutting with Dennis, and when Dad told him he had to pick he just said no and ran off. Dad would chase after him with a piece of hop bine, but Barry didn't care. I can see my father now, chasing him through the rows, shouting and ranting at him, kicking bits of picked bine aside as he chased him. Barry was much too quick for Dad, though. He ran to the top of the rows and dove head first into the pokes of hops just to taunt Dad.

He knew that they wouldn't make a full measure if he dived on them. The hops just went to powder if they got squashed. Dad yelled, "I bet I tan yer, my boy, if I get me hands on yer, you see if I don't." Barry laughed and stuck out his tongue at him in defiance. To make matters worse, the Londoners laughed at Dad as he got so angry with him. Mum smiled to herself as she watched them, and Dad blamed her for all Barry's bad behaviour.

About four o'clock, Barry and Dennis would disappear and all you could hear was their mothers calling them to come home with us. They hid out until we all went home and then they crept out of hiding and sneaked onto the wagon. They knew it was wrong for them to get on it but they didn't care.

At the end of the day, the Hampshire wagon was stacked high each end with the pokes of hops. All you could see were two heads poking out between the pokes, one dark haired and one fair. I'm sure the men knew that they were there, but they made out they didn't and when the cart slowed down as it reached the forge at the top of the lane that went to Hay Place Farm, two small boys slid off the back of it and scuttled up the dip, laughing for all they were worth. The cart would then go on its way to be relieved of its load, then make the return journey to the stables where the horses where unharnessed and fed by Bill, the carter.

THE HOP KILN

I only ever went into the hop kiln once, as children were forbidden to go in there. My father was late home from work and so my mother sent me to see what was keeping him so long. I crossed the fields to the black chicken hut, climbed over the stile and took the shortcut around the potato field. I slid down the embankment in front of the Golding's where the Durman's lived. I could see Tom working hard in his garden. It had rained frequently on and off during the day so the men were working late to make up for it.

I could see my father talking to one of the men. I called out to him. "Dad, Dad, Mum said when ya coming home?"

"Hush," he replied. "Can't yer see I'm talking."

The man he was talking to smiled at me. "It's all right, Charlie, it is late," he said. I stood watching the large pokes of hops going into the kiln. I had never seen what happened to the hops once they had been picked.

"Why are the hops going up on that thing, Dad?" I asked. The hops were put on a kind of slide that went up instead of down.

"You don't want ter know that," said Dad. "Come on, we best be getting back to the huts."

"But. Dad, I want to see," I cried. "I want ter know what's gonna happen to them."

"Take her in, Charlie," said the man that Dad had been talking to. "But keep an eye on her." He smiled at me.

"Well thank the man," said Dad. "Children ain't supposed to come in here you know." As we went in, I could feel the overwhelming heat, and there was a strong smell of sulphur in the air, it took my breath away.

"Ain't it hot in ere, Dad," I said. "Why is it so hot?"

"It's gotta be this hot, the hops won't dry out if it ain't," said Dad. "See up there," he said, pointing to a ladder. "That's the way to the drying rooms up top."

"Can I go up and see?" I asked.

"No," he replied. "You'd roast alive if I took yer up there, and besides, the fumes are enough to kill yer."

"What's that smell?" I asked.

"Sulphur," said Dad. "They put it on the hops in the drying rooms. See that man over there? He's breaking up the sticks of it." The man was crushing up long sticks of sulphur; they looked just like candles except they were yellow. Hearing a clanging sound, I turned to face it. Right behind me was a metal cage. It had weights each side of it and, just as I was wondering what it could be, there was a rushing sound as hops came spewing out of a shoot that was pointing downwards from the ceiling. They were going into a metal cage and a long sack. The weights were then lowered each side of it so as to compress the dried hops inside it. The cage was then opened and the long sack taken out.

"Why is that sack long and why ain't it fat like the pokes?" I asked.

Dad laughed. "You do ask some questions," he said. "It wouldn't go in that cage if it was fat, would it now, and besides it ain't a sack, it's called a pocket."

205

A hoist was used to remove the pocket from the metal cage to where the men were painting on the letters of Hay Place Farm. It was put-on by a stencil in big bold letters with the date and name of the farm, and although it was now Paul's farm it was still called Hay Place. "Come on," said Dad. "I think you've seen enough for one day. It's time we went home for some grub."

"But, Dad, where are the hops going?" I asked. "What's gonna happen to them now?"

"How the hell should I know?" said Dad. "You do ask some funny questions at times." He went on to say, "I expect they're going to the brewery and I think Courage's ave got one out this way. Some of the men from the village work in it, so Tom says. Now, let's get back to the huts, I'm starved."

I couldn't wait to tell Charlie that I had been in the hop kiln. Just wait till I tell him just wait, I thought. I couldn't understand why they made beer from hops as they tasted bitter to me, so I couldn't see how people could drink anything that was made from them.

As we went out, I punched one of the pockets. Dad laughed as I cried out in pain. "You thought that them pockets were soft like the pokes, didn't yer," he said. "You thought they were soft," he laughed. The pockets were as hard as bricks. It gave me quite a shock. We would be going home in just a few days, and the thought of it filled me with sadness. I wished I lived on Hay Place farm as if I did, I would never go to school I hated it.

I was going to have to return to that new school that I so hated. It hadn't been as bad in the other school as I was in the same class as my cousin, Carrie. She lived the other end of Hersham and had not been put in the same school as me. At least back then I had Carrie to go to school with all those other years, but now I had to face the teachers by myself. I was the only child in my school that went hop picking and I knew I could be in trouble, I just knew it. I could hardly wait for the last week in August and I used to wait for the letter in the post each day. When it came, I was packed and ready in no time ready to go. Mum was still having her usual moan about it but my father didn't care. Charlie had started work now so he would only be down at the weekends and for one week's holiday. Charlie worked for the council as an apprentice; he was going to be a painter and decorator. It was the only job he liked that he could get that he didn't have to read or write to do it. He still worked for Uncle Sammy on the fair and he did a log round with him during the winter.

SHANE

This year on arriving everyone was surprised to see that we had a large dog with us, a collie dog, just like the dog, Lassie. Charlie had brought it out of the money he had saved. The dog's name was Shane, and although he was Charlie's, he took no notice of him at all.

Shane sat next to Coral all day long because, as far as he was concerned, she was his master. Charlie kept on impressing on her that the dog was his, but it made no difference to her or the dog. Shane was such a big dog, all sable and white. He had a big white ruff around his neck and a long flowing tail. Charlie hadn't been able to keep him at my aunts, so we had to take him with us. The other pickers were amazed when they saw him. "Where did yer get that dog?" they asked as Dad got him off the lorry.

"I'll give yer a fiver fer it," said a man, holding out a five-pound note to Dad. He waved it about temptingly at my father.

"Leave off," said Dad. "You can't ave im, he cost too much fer the likes of you."

The man took out another crumpled note from his back pocket. "I'll give yer a tenner then."

"He ain't fer sale," shouted Charlie. "That's my dog and he ain't fer sale ,so keep yer money, I don't want it."

The man laughed and, ignoring Charlie, he asked Dad once more. He was a scruffy little man. He had come from one of the tents or caravans that were out in the field.

"That dog's mine," shouted Charlie, "and I got the bill of sale to prove it. You stick yer money. I worked a whole year fer that dog and he's mine." Charlie looked defiantly at Dad. "You can't sell that dog like yer sold my dog, Toby. He's mine and I got the papers to say so," he said. "I got his pedigree." Dad walked away and the little scruffy man left.

Uncle Albert was unloading his boxes and putting them in his hut. He came out of his hut and sat down on an old army bed in the cookhouse. "What's Charlie on about Uncle Albert?" I asked. "What dog?"

"Well, girl," he said. "A long time ago, when you were about six or seven, yer Dad had a bit too much to drink on the way down to Hampshire and he had a bet with a man in the Horseshoe pub. He bet him a ton of money that he could earn more money than he did hopping. Yer dad lost his bet and so he had ter give the man the boy's dog as he never had enough to pay him. Yer poor brother broke his heart when the man dragged the dog off im."

"Yeah," said Charlie, "he took me dog off with a lump of orange box string round its neck." Charlie left, whistling to Shane as he went in the hut.

Uncle Albert shook his head and said, "I never see a boy cry like he did, it broke his heart it did. He kicked the man all up the legs when he dragged it away from him. The man could see he was upset about it so he gave him a hand full of money for it. Charlie threw it back at him. There was money all over the road. I shall never forget it," he said. Now I knew why, when we had arrived home one year minus the dog, no one wanted to talk about it. I also understood why Charlie kept Shane's papers on him all the time now. He was afraid that Dad would sell him, and as he was only coming down for the week and weekends, he wasn't about to take any chances.

Michael ran off with our Barry as soon as we had got off the lorry. Uncle Sammy laughed. "A fat lot of work you're gonna get out of im. He can't wait ter run off. He ain't gonna be any help with the unpacking, I can see."

I looked around the cookhouse. It was just the same. I could still see our ashes in the fireplace from last year. Uncle Albert had his fire on the go and he was already making a cup of tea. Uncle Sammy had a quick cup with Aunt Ivy and then left. Michael wasn't all that popular with the other children as he was such a tell-tale tit. He just couldn't keep his mouth shut and the children took an instant dislike to him. I was always in trouble whenever he was around.

On one occasion, he told Dad that I was with a load of boys with cheese cutters and my father refused to let me out for a week. I had been to a church show and was walking home with June Steelwell when Dad came across the field and dragged me off home. I didn't know what I was supposed to have done and it wasn't until I got back that I found out. "You'll get cut to bits with them boys," said Dad. "I heard tell they had cheese cutters. I don't want yer out after dark with a load of boys."

"What is he on about?" I asked my mum. "What's cheese cutters?" Barry laughed. "He means their caps, that's what cheese cutters are." He went on to say, "Michael told Dad you were with a crowd of boys with cheese cutters, and Dad thinks they're knives. He don't know that they're caps." He fell on Mum's bed laughing for all he was worth.

"Don't take notice of yer dad," said Mum. "He'll forget all about it in a few days." He might, I thought, but I shan't. He had made me look such a fool in front of my friends as well as June's aunt. She had been walking just behind me, and Dad hadn't seen her in the dark. I never spoke to my father for a week or more after that, and as for big mouth

Michael, no one would speak to him. He wasn't any good at picking either as all he wanted to do was go nutting in the woods. Dad said he wouldn't take him any more as he cost more to feed than he was worth.

THE ROUGH GYPSIES ARE BACK

Mum wasn't all that happy once she saw that the rough gypsies were back. "I won't be able to hang a bit of washing out," she said, "not now that lot's ere."

"We better keep an eye on the wood, too," said Uncle Albert. "That lot'll take it all if we don't watch em."

"I best tie the dog to the bavins fer a few days," said Dad. "They won't want ter touch the wood or anything else if the dog's here."

They left us alone until about a week later. We arrived at the huts to find the dog missing. "That's funny," said Dad. "I wonder where the dog is, it's not like him to run off." He went all over Hay Place whistling and calling, but got no reply. "That's strange, that dog would never have gone on his own. Someone must ave taken im. He wouldn't leave my Coral."

"I bet that lot ave got im," said Uncle Albert. "I'd stake me life on it."

"Yes," Uncle Horace replied. "I bet I know where he is all right." Coral cried and cried. Mum didn't know what to do with her as she and the dog were inseparable.

Dad let it be known that he was going to the police. He said that he would have them search all the huts and caravans for the dog. "If my dog ain't back ere by tonight," he said, "I'm going fer the gavers." He said it in earshot of the scruffy little man that tried to buy the dog on the day we arrived. That night the dog was back.

"I thought that would do the trick," said Uncle Albert "They don't want the gavers searching their places."

"They got too much to hide fer that," said Uncle Horace. "I bet they had im locked up and muzzled in one of them caravans." They kept well away from us after that as they knew that we were wise to them.

CORAL

Shane sat by my sister, Coral, all day; they lay dozing in the sun tied up to the same hop bine. Dad had tied them to it to stop them from running off, as they did so whenever they had the chance to. People thought it so funny to see them as they were such an unusual sight. Coral lay fast asleep with her head between his front paws and the dog stayed in that position until she woke up.

Mum would have let her wander about if it weren't for the dip at the edge of the hop garden. Bull Pit was at the edge and just a thin line of trees separated it from the steep drop on the other side. Bull Pit was a crater I think; it was not man-made, I'm sure. It made an ideal hop garden as it was sheltered from the wind. My mother was so afraid that my sister would fall in it and break her neck. My cousin, Louie, had fallen in it when she was small and the pole pullers had to pull her out with their long poles. The only way down into it was a steep cart track. When my brother and I were small, my mother told us that the trees had snakes in them and that if we went too close to the dip we would fall in and the snakes would eat us. Although we were now older and knew better, we still shivered at the thought of it.

Dad spoilt Coral something rotten. She had her own way all the time, a bit like Mum with Barry.

I was unable to pick half the time as I spent most of my time looking after Coral. If it rained, I had to stop at the huts with her as she was a very sickly child. Mum wouldn't let her get wet if she could help it. Dad was just as bad. He made me stay back at the huts until later in the day when the rain had eased up and I was then allowed to bring her out to the hop fields. They didn't take her out in the early morning mist like they did with us. No, she was proper spoilt and pampered all the time.

I don't know where she got her temper from, but it was dreadful. She would go stiff as a plank when I was sent to get her in for her tea at tea time and then go purple in the face because she screamed so much.

Sometimes she passed out and I got into trouble for letting her get into such a state. "She wants a good smack," said Uncle Albert. "I'd bet I'd stop her antics is she was mine." I was expected to watch her all the time, no matter what, but I found a way around it.

The Caerys had a daughter with learning difficulties, her name was Becky. Becky loved to play with Coral and, as no one else would play with her, she was only too happy to play with Coral. The boys all laughed at Becky and called her nasty names; they were so unkind to her. She was always giving them her apples and her cakes so as she could join in, but they just took what she gave them then told her to shove off.

I wondered where she was getting all the things she was giving Barry and Dennis one day, as when she had passed me, she had nothing in her hands. She was talking to Coral as she pushed her around the huts in her pram. Barry and Dennis stopped her and demanded that she get them some apples. I watched as she went to the side of our hut and took two big red apples from her knicker leg. I couldn't believe it when she gave them one each. I waited until they had each taken a bite before telling them what she had done. "You know where Becky got them apples, you're eatin, don't yer. She had em in her drawers." You should have seen their faces. Dennis almost choked and Barry went mad. They spat out the apples and ran for the tap to wash their mouths out. I couldn't stop laughing.

Mum asked what was going on and I told her. She then had a good laugh as well. "Serve em right," she said. "That'll teach em to laugh at that poor girl and poke fun at her. She can't help the way she is." I never saw them take anything from her ever again after that.

PEACHES AND CREAM

Charlie came down at the weekends and kept a close watch on Dad. I don't think he trusted him all that much. He would pat his breast pocket and say, "I got the papers on me so yer can't sell me dog, he ain't no good for sale without these." I kept out of Charlie's way if I could as he never lost the chance to get me into trouble.

I sat in the barn with Vera and plastered on some face powder. "Mmm, this is nice," I said. "What's it called?"

"Peaches and Cream," she replied "It's a new face powder from Rubenstein's. Louie got a big bag full of it." How grown up I felt as I gazed at my reflection in the compact mirror. Charlie spotted me, though, and revelled in telling Dad.

"'Im telling Dad you got make up all over yer face, I am, don't you fret."

"Big mouth," I yelled back at him. "Tell him then, see if I care, boily nose." Charlie had a big boil at the end of his nose and no matter how much he tried, he couldn't shift it. He tried all sorts of creams and lotions but it wouldn't go. He was very touchy about it and I knew it. He took a dive at me and I ran, but in my haste to get away from him I ran across the yard straight into the cow dung. I stood ankle deep in it screaming for Mum. What a sight I must have been.

Vera came out of the barn laughing for all she was worth. "You look a proper mess," she said. "I don't know about Peaches and Cream, you smell more like a cow shed to me. Give me your sandals and I'll wash em fer yer."

Charlie sauntered off to the cookhouse laughing at my discomfort.

A FULL MEASURE

Measuring the hops never lost its fascination for me. Dad was a pole puller and he helped with the measuring. It took four men to measure the hops, two of them to hold the poke of hops and two to hold the measure basket. The hops were tipped from a poke into a measuring basket and then, when it was a full measure, they were put back into the poke and left for the men to collect when the cart came at the end of a day's picking.

Tom marked the picker's cards and then wrote an entry in his green ledger. Two men walked behind the cart as it came down the roadway. They then dragged out the pokes from the rows and then with their long steel needles they stitched up the necks of the pokes with string. Then with two metal hand hooks, the men dragged the pokes across the roadway and swung them high in the air to the two men who were on the back of the cart. The men stacked the hops into the back of the cart and so it went on, all along the hop rows, until the cart was full. Now that the farm no longer used horses to work on it, tractors were used, the familiar sound of the tramping hooves gone forever. In their place was the sound of the tractor's faltering engine spluttering and coughing as it tried in vain to pull its heavy load up Bull Pit's steep slope.

Dad laughed. "Serve em right," he said. "They should er kept the old horses and they wouldn't ave all this palaver each time it rains, would they, Alb."

Uncle Albert nodded in agreement. "They ave to get the Land Rover," he said. "They won't shift if they don't. Them old horses couldn't last fer ever though. We must move with the times, Chat. We can't stand still forever, ya know."

Dad shook his head. It had broken his heart when he found out that the farm had done away with horses in favour of tractors. Dad resented any sort of change at the farm. I think that he felt that it should stay the same as it was when he was a boy. He stood and watched as the tractor was winched from the slope with the help of the Land Rover from the farm. I don't think he liked the fumes from the diesel, he said it stank. "Horses don't stink," he said to Mum. "But yer know it when yer follow the cart now they got that stinking thing."

Mum laughed. "You just didn't like to see the horses go, that's your trouble, Charlie Ayres."

RAY DURMAN

Ray Durman loved our dog and the dog loved him. He didn't go for Ray like he did most other people. Ray would poke his head around our hut door at night and stroke his head. "That's what I call a dog," he said. "Not like ours."

"What's wrong with your dog?" said Mum. "He's a nice little dog."

Ray laughed. "The bloody thing wants shooting. He bites Peter and me, he nips us in the ankles when Mum's not looking. I hate im."

Mum laughed. "I don't think yer old mum would like that, not one bit."

Ray laughed once more. "Do ya want anything from the post office, Mrs Ayres?" he asked. "I can go on me bike and get it fer yer."

Mum smiled. "No, my sunshine, I've been already, thanks all the same."

Turning towards me he asked, "Are you going to the barn, the others are in there."

"Go on," said Mum, "you can go out."

We crossed the yard and went into the barn. I could hear the others but couldn't see them. Suddenly my cousin, Vera, poked her head over the top of a stack of hay. "What yer doing?" I asked. "What's going on?"

"Peter Durman's giving the girls kissing lessons," she said. "Come and see."

Ray turned and went out.

"What's up, Durmy?" Peter shouted. Ray told him to shut up. Then Peter made a grab for me. Holding me down, he kissed me hard on the mouth. I spat at him. "You dirty bitch," he yelled. "No call to do that, was there."

I ran from the barn after Ray as fast as I could. I think Peter did it so as to make Ray angry. He knew the pickers liked Ray more than him. Besides, Ray was mother's little Ray of sunshine, so in her eyes he could do no wrong.

MRS PRITCHARD THE LONDONER

That night, I sat in the cookhouse with Ray, Dennis, Barry and some of the others. Louie and Vera came in laughing. "What's up?" I asked.

"Mrs Pritchard," said Vera. "Ave yer seen her?" The Londoners had all cooked their food so the cookhouse was empty. We could never sit in ours and talk because Uncle Albert wouldn't let us. We were all taking when Mrs Pritchard's daughter came in. She sat talking to the rest of us about London. Her name was Margaret. She was quite small with dark hair and big brown eyes. She was also a year or so older than us, but her mother never let her out. Mrs Pritchard shouted for her to go in. Marching into the cookhouse, she marched Margaret out.

"Didn't you hear me, Margaret? I called and called for ya to come in." She returned a few minutes later. She picked up a kettle, grunted and went out. Barry, Ray and Dennis followed her, mocking the way she walked. She almost caught them when she turned to go into her hut. We were all sniggering and laughing at her. I don't think that she ever wore women's clothes, as she only wore a long land army coat over her dungarees, the bottoms tucked inside her wellies. She had turned down the tops of them to reveal a pair of men's army socks. We laughed so much that she almost caught us.

"I think she might be a man," said Ray.

"She talks like one," said Dennis, laughing. "Yes, she must be, she has a moustache. Avent yer seen, it avent yer noticed? Margaret! Margaret!" he mimicked, as he strode about pretending to be her. What a laugh it was when she came in and almost caught him.

After the boys went home, Vera, Louie and me sat in the cookhouse talking. "I wonder if she is a man," said Vera. "I wonder if she's got hair all over her." I thought that I was hearing things, well I hoped I was.

I had forgotten all about Mrs Pritchard until the next night. Vera came for me to go to the toilet with her, as we always went in pairs. The toilets had no windows in them and no light, so we didn't like to go alone. I had completely forgotten our conversation of the previous night, that was, until I saw Mrs. Pritchard going into the lavatory. She went into the first one by the door. It was the lightest one. The toilet had no windows in it as it was just as primitive as the old one. There was a semi-partition between the two that did not quite go to the end. We hadn't got a torch with us and it was getting very dark. Vera started to laugh as she climbed up on to the toilet seat and she tried to peep around the end of the partition, when suddenly she lost her footing and almost fell down the toilet. I begged her to get down but she wouldn't hear of it. At one point she lost her boot down the toilet.

"Please get down, Vera," I begged. "She might see yer if yer don't."

We made such a noise that Mrs Pritchard did hear us; well, she saw me. "I see you, miss," she yelled. "I know ya Charlie's girl." We fled from that toilet as fast as we could, but I was not quick enough. She grabbed me by the scruff of the neck as I tried to run past her door. "Got ya," she said as she boxed my ears. I struggled like mad but she held me fast. "I'll ave to tell ya father of this," she said, "you rude girl."

Suddenly I was free, my ears stinging from the clout she had just given me. I ran to our cookhouse to find Vera laughing fit to bust. "You should see yer face, it's all red like a beetroot."

"Well, yours would be red if she had hit you," I retorted. "She's going to tell me dad it was me that was spying on her. It's all right fer you," I shouted. "Go on tell her, tell her it wasn't me. Go on."

"No," said Vera. "Then she'll know it was me and she'll tell my dad and then I'll be the one that gets hit."

"Well, what about me then?" I asked. "What will I do if my dad finds

223

out about it?" Vera sat there laughing as she couldn't have cared less. "That's the last time I ever go to the toilet with you," I said. "I don't see why I should take the blame for what you do." Vera laughed. "Did yer see if she was a man?" I asked.

"No," replied Vera, in between her rolling laughter. "It was too dark to see."

With stinging ears, I went into our hut. I had hoped Mum wouldn't notice my red ears as she would have been very cross with me even though I hadn't done anything. Just being with Vera was enough to get me a good hiding.

MY MOTHER'S PAST

The following night, as I walked towards our hut, I could see my mother washing in the little tin bath tub. She stood rubbing a shirt up and down the scrubbing board in an effort to get it clean. She stopped from time to time to push a stray curl back underneath her headscarf. "Oh, I hate hopping," she moaned. "I hate washing in this thing," she said wearily. "I'm so tired and I do miss my old boiler."

Wiping her hands on her apron, she came into the hut and flopped on the bed. "What's wrong, Mum?" I asked.

"What's wrong?" she asked in amazement. "What's wrong? I'll tell yer what's wrong I thought that when I married yer father, I would be able to settle down, not go traipsing all this way each year to live like pigs." She gave a deep sigh. "I had enough of this sort of life when I was a child," she said. "I don't want to live like this year after year. It's all right fer yer dad, he can sit in the pub or else he's in that cookhouse talking half the night with the men. He ain't gotta wash clothes or cook grub like me. Oh no, he don't care. I always wanted a home of me own, so as I could settle down when I was married. I had enough of this way of life when we were all at home. Why do ya think I got married?" she went on to say. "Yer Granny was in the circus in her younger days. She walked the wires, yer know." Mum gave a feeble little smile. "Yer grandmother was a tight rope walker when she was a young girl and yer Uncle Tommy a lion tamer."

"You mean you were with the circus," I cried, not believing my ears.

"Yes," said Mum. "It's not all fun, though. Its hard work, I can tell yer." I knew that my mother's people came from fair grounds, but had no idea it was the circus as well. How exciting, I thought. "Yes," said Mum. "I remember when we were all small, my sisters, brothers and me went all over the country with the circus. "I saw my Uncle Tommy mauled to death in front of me by his lion, Leo, it was awful. He had an act where he put his head in its mouth and he did all sorts of tricks with it. One night when he was just coming to the end of his act, he accidentally hit the lion on his back with his wooden leg. It pounced on him and mauled him. They never shot the lion as it was Uncle Tommy's dying wish that they let the lion live." Mum shook her head. "Yer granny married beneath her, so her family thought when she married your grandfather, Albert. He was just a hired hand at the time and they never forgave her for running away with him to get married. They wanted her to marry a mill owner's son who was in love with her. She could have had anything she wanted if she had married him. My poor old mum," she said with a sigh.

"You were lucky, Mum," I said. "Fancy being with the circus."

She sighed once more. "I had to go into service," she said. "I had to leave home when I was fourteen. I wasn't any older than you when my brother, Sammy, threw me out."

"Why did he do that?" I asked. "What did your Mum and Dad say?"

"They couldn't say anything," she said. "Yer grandfather had a poisoned leg and couldn't work. Yer granny had just had another baby and with all the other mouths to feed, she had to rely on yer Uncle Sammy as he was the bread winner. Uncle Sammy had come back from a tarmacking job to see us as he had news that his father was unable to look after us. He had heard this from a local man. He found us all starving and neither of our parents could earn enough to buy as much as a crust of bread. Sammy took over and run the place. We had to do as he said or else. He wouldn't let us out unless it was fer work in the laundry, and when we got our money, he took it and wouldn't even let us go to the pictures." Mum went on to say, "We went out one night, my sister, Annie, and me. We had some extra money for working late so we went to the pictures. We tried to get back in our caravan without Sammy hearing us. We was all right till the bloody dog barked. It woke Uncle Sammy and there was all hell to pay. Yer granny knew we was out but she had told him that we had all took an early night when he got in from work. Sammy thought us to all be in bed. When he saw us, he ordered us out there and then. He said that we would all come home with a bundle in our arms and bring shame on the family, so we had to go or he wouldn't stay."

"Oh, Mum, what did you do?" I asked. "Where did yer go?"

"We all went into service," she said. "We had to split up and work for different people. We had to make our own way in life." Leaning forward she brushed the hair back from my face. "You're just like my Annie," she said in a sad voice. "You certainly don't take after me or yer father, that's fer sure."

"Who's Annie?" I asked.

"Annie was my sister. She went missing after we girls went into service and I ain't heard from her from that day to this. You got her small features," she said, brushing my hair from my face once more. "I often wondered what become of her. I expect she's dead as if she wasn't I would ave heard from her by now, I know I would. Me and my Annie were close, we was, we were like that." Mum crossed her two fingers. "You remind me so much of my Annie, you got her features all right." Mum went on to say, "I wanted to call you Annie, but yer dad said no. That's why you have three names, Sheila Judith Anne. Yer dad said it would be unlucky fer me to name yer after her. Annie wanted me to marry a young musician that was sweet on me at the time." Mum's eyes threatened to brim over at any moment. "She didn't want me to marry yer father. She said I would end up like Ivy, broke, with half a dozen kids." The tears that Mum had tried so hard to stop were running down her cheeks. Getting up, she returned to her washing, dabbing her eyes on the corner of her scarf.

"This is our holiday though, Mum," I said. Turning to face me, she replied, "It might be your idea of one, but it's not mine. All I ever do is slog me guts out from morning to night. It's not what I want a holiday to be like, no not at all. You're too small to understand. Go to bed, it's late."

I lay in my bed conjuring up all sorts of pictures in my mind. I tried to picture my aunt. I wondered what had become of her. I could see now why my mother hated to come hop picking, as it was nothing but hard work for her, but for me it was the most exciting time of my young life, one that would remain engraved on my mind and heart.

SECRET MEETINGS

The next night, Ray, Edie, Vera and I crept into the barn. We had been told to keep out of there by Tom as it wasn't safe any more. The tiles kept falling through the roof and the rafters were rotten. We sneaked in through the little door that went into the tackroom as we could get into the stables from there. We thought that we were so clever. We didn't know that my sister had seen us and she went and told Charlie.

Mmm, what you got on?" said Ray.

Vera laughed. "Peaches and cream," she shouted.

"Peaches and what?" said Ray. We all laughed.

"Peaches and Cream, it's face powder. Ain't yer ever heard of face powder?"

The boys laughed, they didn't believe us, I just knew they didn't. We sat with our arms around each other, talking about our schools and how we got on during the year when we got home. Ray and Eddy said they got caned for staying away from school when we hop pickers came, because they were always taking time off when they should have been in school. "The place is dead when you pickers go home," they said. "The huts are empty and the pubs are just the same."

"I hate it when you go home,"said Ray. "There's nothing going on, it's dead like the grave."

We didn't hear Charlie enter as he had sneaked in through the barn and had been spying on us all the time. He stood with his arms folded across his chest. "I'm telling Dad you're in this barn with these boys," he said. "And he'll make yer scrub all that shit off yer face, old gel. Peaches and Cream, who ever heard of such muck."

He swiped out at me and I ran from the barn shouting for Mum, but not before I shouted back at him. "You're such a big man, Charlie Ayres, it's such a shame you weren't such a big man when you were Binstead's Champion fighter, isn't it."

He ran after me, threatening all sorts of dire things as well as calling me haystack head. "Go on, stick yer head over the fence and give the cows a good feed," he shouted. "Go on, give em a treat. That's not hair on yer head, it's hay."

"Can't yer leave the gel alone?" said Uncle Albert as he stood by the wall in front of the huts. "You're do her damage if yer keep hitting her like yer do, boy, yer ain't supposed to hit gels." Charlie sauntered off and Uncle Albert turned to me and said, "I should get all that muck off yer face if I was you, Sheila, before yer father sees it. I don't think he'll take too kindly to you wearing that muck. Get and wash it off, and tell that Vera that I've seen her as well, don't you fret."

We washed it off, expecting him to tell our dads but he never did. We still sneaked into the barn during the days at the weekends when Charlie wasn't around, and we walked down the lane to Hay Place Farm in the moonlight. Sometimes we would stop in the roadway below the Steelwell's hut and listen to them talking. We could hear June telling her aunt about Dennis because he kept spying on her through a knot hole in the partition that separated their huts. Their huts had two bedrooms in them and they had stacks of furniture. Although they were chicken huts on the inside, they were nothing like it. They even had a wireless with them. Dennis and June could listen to *Journey into Space* and they would let Barry in to listen to it. Barry took great delight in telling us all about it. We laughed as we stood listening and we were to laugh a lot more when June's aunt threw a bucket of water down the bank onto the roadway below, where we were standing. Ray got covered.

"I hope that's water and not something else," said Eddy, laughing as Ray sniffed at it.

"It had better be water," replied Ray. "It bloody well better be."

ALBERT AND EADIES WEDDING

On the following Saturday, my mother and father went away, leaving
Barry and I in Charlie's care. All my aunts and uncles went too. I believe
a friend of my mother's had Coral. They all came back late that night. I
asked them where they had been. "We bin to Albert and Edie's wedding,"
said Dad. "They was married today."

"But, Mum," I cried. "They can't be, they just can't."

"Why?" said Dad laughing.

"I can assure you they were," said Mum. "We was there."

"But, Mum," I cried. "I was supposed to be Edie's bridesmaid. They
just can't be married, no, not without me."

Charlie laughed. "What makes you think they would want a fat ugly
thing like you?" he asked "Who wants a thing like you with a haystack
for a head in their photographs."

"But Albert promised I was going to be one of his bridesmaids, he
promised," I sobbed.

"Well you ain't," said Charlie. "So there, fancy a big old gel like you crying, you big baby."

I ran from the hut to the barn; I could always think better in there. How could he break his promise to me like that, I thought? How could he. I heard a lot of laughter coming from the huts so I went to see just what was going on. Wiping my eyes, I walked towards Aunt Liza's hut, as I could see a large crowd by the door. I could hear Edie's voice above all the commotion, begging to be let out of Aunt Liza's hut. Suddenly, Uncle Bill Burden opened the hut door and dragged her from it.

"What's up?" he asked. "Is that old army bed too hard fer yer gel? I know what yer wants, yer wants yer Aunt Mima's brass bed, don't yer." He shoved Edie and Albert along the huts, with Edie hanging on to Albert for all she was worth. "There," he said, as he pushed them into our hut. "Get on with it. We won't watch, we'll go in the cookhouse. Just look at what yer Aunt Mima got fer sleeping on, that old brass bed." He was pointing to Coral. How mum blushed when the others began laughing.

"Let us out, Aunt Mima," they begged, but she was too frightened of Bill to do so.

"Let the poor girl out, Bill," she said. "You'll frighten her stiff, she's not used to you like we are."

"Well, she'll just ave ter get used to me," he said. "She's one of the family now, she just better get used to it." He walked away laughing. When Bill finally let them out, they emerged from the hut red faced and very angry.

Edie kept well out of his way after that, as she was so frightened of him.

"I can't ave my relations sleeping apart on their honeymoon," he said. "It ain't right, is it now." It had been Albert's suggestion that he and Edie spend their honeymoon at the huts, as all their money had been spent on the wedding. Albert thought that they could earn a little spending money. The only thing was, they hadn't got a hut. So, Edie had to sleep with Aunt Liza and Albert slept with his brother, Henry, and his father, Albert, in Henry's hut. Edie had never picked a hop in her life and had no idea at all on how to do it. What a laugh it was when she tried to pick hops. Uncle Albert went barmy. Edie was picking them one at a time, much to our amusement.

"Look," said Uncle Albert. "That's how yer do it." Edie just looked at him. "You'll be ere till Christmas if yer pick em like that, gel," he said. "For Christ's sake, move yer self. Look, watch me, girl." Snapping off a branch of hops, he stripped the leaves from it and then scooped the hops in the palm of his hand in one go, scattering the hops into the basket. "There," he said. "That's how it's done, not one at a time, gel."

Mum and Dad laughed as they could see how frustrated my uncle was getting. At one point, I thought he was going to hit her because she was picking so slow. I know Edie didn't like hop picking as I heard her tell my mum. She didn't like the taste of them on her food and she couldn't get the hop stains from her hands, this upset her.

"This is the last time I pick hops," she said. "Just look at my hands, they're red raw and my hair's all over the place. I can't do a thing with it, Aunt Mima."

Mum laughed. "You're get used to it, my luv," she said, "and I can lend you a head scarf to stop yer hair blowing all over the place."

I could tell that this would be the last time that Edie would come as her heart was not in it, and she didn't expect to not be sleeping with her husband, Albert. I thought it would be the last year for Albert, as well, as he had been put off by his father. Albert had been forced to pick since he was small; this held no fondness for him. My uncle had been a hard taskmaster to his children.

MUM'S DRIVING LESSON

My mother was moaning one Saturday about waiting for the little bus that took her to Alton to get her shopping. "I do wish I could drive," she said. "I'm so fed up with having to wait fer that old bone shaker.

"What's wrong, Mima?" Uncle Albert asked.

"Don't take no notice of her, Albert," said Dad. "She's always got to moan about something or other."

"So would you moan if you was me," said Mum. "You don't ave ter go in the old bone shaker all the way to Alton, and lug shopping, oh no. I'd like to see you wait fer that bus fer an hour or more with a bag full of shopping, I bet you wouldn't like it."

"You don't ave to go be bus, Mima," said Uncle Albert. "I'll take yer."

Mum laughed. "You must be joking," she said, "if yer think I'd get in a car with you, Albert." The other pickers laughed; they knew well enough that my mother didn't trust Uncle Albert's driving as she said so often enough.

My Uncle Bill Burden had been listening to their conversation. Getting up, he came over to Mum. "There's a car out there, Mima," he said. "Drive yerself." The other men in the cookhouse began to snigger.

"Very well, Bill, "she said. "You teach me."

The look on my father's face was a picture. He was so shocked that she had asked Bill to show her how to drive. I must say I was rather surprised myself.

Uncle Bill sat next to Mum in the front of the car and Dad and my sister, Coral, sat in the back. Off they went, the car going up and down like a kangaroo. There were cows out in the field when she took off, but they soon disappeared running in all directions.

A poor horse tethered out in the middle of the field went mad trying to get away from her as she seemed to be mesmerised by it. She kept on going around in circles, following the poor thing's tail. How the pickers laughed. Dad was a white as a sheet. He sat holding the back of her seat, screaming at her to stop, and my sister clung to him. As she finally brought the car to a standstill, a large crowd cheered and shouted, "Well done, Mima, well done." Dad stumbled from the car looking as though he were about to throw up at any moment. Coral stood at his side, clinging on to him for all she was worth and Uncle Bill could do nothing for laughing as Mum walked away.

"Who's a mad driver now?" asked Uncle Albert as she passed him in the cookhouse on her way to our hut. Mum walked straight by him, her head held high as she went into our hut.

Dad came in. "You best get the bus to Alton, Mima," he said, "because you will never make a driver and that's fer sure."

"I drove, didn't I?" she said. "That showed you a thing or two, Ayres. I could drive if I wanted to, I just don't like the roads, that's all."

THE TAR WELL

One night, as we arrived back after a hard day's work, we saw the boys of Eastwood with their dog. Well, I thought it was a dog, but it was hard to tell. It was as black as coal. It had fallen into the tar well. What a sight it was. They put it down and it sat whimpering and whining at their feet, with tar dripping from it. One of the Londoners gave them a tin bath to wash it in. Someone else poured a packet of Lux soap flakes in it and they began to wash it. "You may as well shoot that dog," said one of the pickers. "It will only die after swallowing all that tar, just look at the poor thing."

"You leave me dog alone," shouted Ronnie Eastwood. "You shut yer mouth, it ain't your dog to shoot."

"It's the kindest thing to do," replied the man. "It will only die in agony if yer don't."

"Mum, Mum," screamed Ronnie, "the mush wants ter shoot me dog."

Annie came marching around the corner of the huts, her fist clenched. "What man?" she asked. "Where is he?" Everyone went quiet as they knew what a temper she had. She could fight like a man and she often did.

"That mush said our dog wants shooting," said Henry, or Professor 'H', as Charlie liked to call him.

"Yes," said his brother, Ronnie. "That's im." He pointed at one of the Londoners.

"Oh, did he now," said Annie. "We'll see about that." Rolling back her sleeves, she approached the man.

He backed away from her. "I only meant that it would be the kindest thing to do with it," he said. "That's all. I never meant the boy's dog any harm."

"And who asked fer your opinion?" Annie retorted angrily. "I don't recollect asking you what should be done with my boy's dog." The man backed away as he didn't want to pick a fight with her, as he knew what a bad temper Annie had. She was always fighting with her husband, Perry, and she came off best nine times out of ten.

Over the next few days, that poor dog lost most of its fur. It fell out in clumps. It was Ruff by name and rough by nature. The dog was soon back on form, though, it was fighting with the other dogs as usual. It even had a go at Mrs Durman's little dog which was a Scotch terrier named Bracken. It flew for her dog, dragging it from her arms, and she was so upset about it at the time. The dog had to be taken to the vet as it was so badly hurt. Ruff had bitten it all over. It had terrible cuts and wounds and was suffering from shock. The Eastwoods were told to keep Ruff tied up after that by Mrs Durman, but they didn't take any notice of her. It ran around just the same fighting with all of the dogs except ours. I don't know why but it never went for our dog. He had one fight with Shane and that was enough, I think. Ruff only went for dogs that were afraid of him. He didn't attack dogs that stood their ground like ours. I think Ruff was a cross collie, although it was hard to tell as he was so tatty and dirty, he was a mongrel.

THE HOP PICKING MACHINES ARE COMING

There was an uneasy feeling about the place now as there was talk of hop picking machines. I heard my Uncle Horace talk about the one that Longman's Farm had got.

"What machine?" asked Dad. "What yer on about?"

"Longmans ave got a machine that picks hops," said Uncle Horace. "You comma longa me tonight and I'll show yer."

After tea, Dad went with him to Longmans, returning a short time later. Dad was very angry. He sat down in the cookhouse and shook his head. "Well," said Mum, "can a machine pick hops, Charlie?"

Dad gave a deep sigh. "You should see what that machine is doing to the hops," he said. "It's murderin em."

Uncle Horace laughed. "I told yer there was a machine that picked hops and now perhaps yer will believe me the next time I tell yer something. I bet the new man gets one fer this farm and I bet he won't keep on us pickers." Stands to reason he'll get a machine now that Longmans ave got one."

"Don't talk rot, Horace," said Dad. "Of course he won't."

"Time will tell," said my uncle. "Time will tell."

Dad began to speak again as though he needed to reassure himself. "He won't get a machine, they leave too many leaves and stalks behind," said Dad. "If we left the leaves like that thing does, we would all get sacked."

"What new man?" I asked my father. "Who is Uncle Horace talking about?"

"The farm's bin sold," Dad replied. "Mr Paul is selling it; we shall ave a new man next year. He won't get a new machine though. I heard im tell Mr Paul that he would not do away with us pickers, because we are better than any machine."

"I wouldn't bet on that, Chat," said Uncle Albert. Dad got very angry and walked out.

Uncle Horace laughed. "He believes in everything he hears," he said. "I give this new man one year and then he'll get a machine, no matter what he's told Mr Paul. Stands to reason yer can't compete with a machine, yer gotta move with the times and they is changing fast. Charlie should know that." Uncle Albert nodded in agreement.

My heart sank. All this talk of machines picking hops filled me with dismay, as the thought of not being able to go on my hop picking holiday was more than I could bear. To me it was unthinkable.

THE SICK CHILD

The following night after tea we heard a commotion coming from the back huts on the Londoners' side. "What on earth is the matter?" Mum asked. "What's all the fuss?"

Mrs Simms came out of her hut and spoke to Mum. "It's Nell Murphy, Mima, her littlun's bin rushed to hospital."

"What on earth's the matter with im?" asked Mum.

"I don't know," Mrs Simms replied, "but I think it must be serious or they wouldn't rush the little chap in."

"Well, at least he's in the right place," said Mum.

The next day the child grew worse and Nell Murphy was sent for. Later that night she returned to the huts in a very distressed state. It seemed that the child was so ill that he no longer knew who she was. The hospital thought it best that she returns to the huts as she could do nothing for the child if she remained. How she sobbed when she came back.

"How is he?" the pickers asked. "Is he any better?"

Nell ran into her hut crying. Her friend that had been with her spoke. "He's just like a little angel," she said. "All in his white night shirt, he looks so peaceful in the oxygen tent. They think its pneumonia he's got, but they can't be sure until they do some tests on the poor little mite."

They sent word to Nell Murphy's husband in London to come. When he arrived, my mother tried to reassure them that all would be well. "Perhaps he's got a bad chill like my Barry had one year," she said. "I wouldn't worry too much about it if I were you."

"But what will I do?" said Nell "You all go home soon, the picking's almost at an end. My husband got to go home. I can't stop at the huts all on me own, can I. They say my baby will be in hospital fer weeks and weeks."

After we went home, we were told that Tom and Ivy Durman let Nell Murphy stay at their cottage until the child was well enough to travel home after he came out of hospital, "That was good of Tom and Ivy to

240

do that fer them people," said Dad. "They didn't ave ter do that, yer know. I know he's the foreman but he ain't got ter help the pickers after the picking's over and take em in. Not many people would do that, Alb," he said. My Uncle Albert agreed with him wholeheartedly.

BILL BURDEN

During the year my cousin, Tillie Burden, had died. She had a growth in her stomach and had died as a result of it. My uncle and aunt were still very upset by her sudden death. Uncle Bill would cry at the mention of her name, and although he still joked and fooled around, he no longer had his heart in it. They didn't come hop picking now, but they did come to the farm selling fruit and vegetables by the lorry-load to the pickers.

He would stop by the dip and then ring his bell. You should see us children run, as he said that we had two minutes in which to eat as much as we could, but woe betide us if we ate after that. He had a stick and would hit us with it if we were still on his lorry eating once the time was up. What a sight we made, all shoving and pushing to get at the fruit. "That's it," he said. "Eat all yer can, but don't let me ketch yer when I blow this whistle or else." It was just like my uncle to do a silly thing like that. He was a very strange man in some ways.

Mum was still very nervous of him and she would make sure that Dad was close to hand when she bought fresh vegetables from him. Uncle Bill never lost the chance to taunt her as he knew she was frightened of him. "What's up, Joan?" he would ask. He always called her Joan as that is the name she used when in service. The people she was in service for did not like the name Jemima and would not call her by it. I could never get used to him calling her by that name and I would look around to see who he was talking to whenever he did so. He would put his arms around my mother and my sister, Coral, would scream at him to let her go as she was scared to death of him. Coral would kick him in the leg to make him free Mum and then tug and tug at my mother to get her away from him as soon as she could. Uncle Bill did it all the more as he enjoyed teasing her. Dad just looked on laughing.

Mum got very angry at times and she would moan at him. "A fat lot of good you are, couldn't yer see what he was doing?"

Dad just laughed once more. "He don't mean nothin by it, Mima," he said. "It's all done in jest, that's all."

I could tell Mum wasn't so sure. "Make him stop it," said Mum. "It's embarrassing."

"You ought to know Bill by now, Mima," said Dad. "How can I say anything to him?"

My Aunt Tillie just sat and looked on laughing. She was used to his pranks. he had done them so often before.

GROWING UP

I had to sneak into the barn now as my mother was unhappy about my going in it. She was always telling me to keep out of it. "You're a woman now," she said, "so I don't want to catch yer with them boys." I couldn't for the life of me see what was wrong in going in the barn as I had gone in there so many times before, and she hadn't bothered then. What was she on about, first she tells me I'm a woman and in the next breath I get told I'm still a child? Why was it grown-ups had a way of making life so difficult? All I wanted to do was sit in the barn and talk. I felt very confused as half of me longed to walk the beams and play in the hay, yet the other half wanted to dress up and sit in the cookhouse with the grown-ups. I seemed to have lost my identity and I no longer knew who I was or what I really wanted. I suppose it was all a part of growing up and that all children reach that stage when they are no longer children and yet have not reached adulthood.

Vera and I still went into the barn, though. We sneaked in and sat talking to Ray and Eddy, unbeknown to Mum. We sat in the cookhouse very late on our last night together; we knew it was to be our last night for another year so we tried to make it last as long as we could. We sat talking and laughing trying to be as cheerful as we could, but there were long periods of silence in between the laughter. How I hated this time of each ending year, when it came to the last night before going home. We sat staring into the dying embers of the fire wishing that time would stand still as none of us wanted to leave. Finally, my father called for me to go in so I had to say my goodbyes and go in to bed.

The next day, I helped Mum to pack and sat on the bed reading. I was just able to read now and I did so whenever I got the chance to. However, I could only read very slowly and it took all my concentration to do so.

Ray stood at the hut door, his head bowed. "I'm going now," he said, as he stood shuffling his feet in a nervous manner. Once again, I could hear the sound of the school bus as it beeped at the end of the road. I wasn't paying all that much attention to Ray as whenever I had my head in a book, I was oblivious to anything or anyone. Ray coughed as he shifted from one foot to the other in an attempt to get my attention. I heard the bus beep once more and screech to a halt by the field gate. Ray shouted goodbye and ran down the dip calling, "Bye, Mrs Ayres, see yer next year." It didn't actually sink in that Ray had gone and I wouldn't see him for another year. I was that engrossed in my book.

My mother's voice brought me back to reality. "You are horrible to that boy. All yer can do is stick yer head in that book. He only wanted to say goodbye to you, that's all, poor little sod."

I ran from the hut calling his name. "Ray, Ray, wait." But it was too late, the bus was already out of sight. As I climbed up the dip, I tore up the book I was reading in frustration.

"It's no use you doing that," said Mum. "You should have been listening when he was ere," she taunted.

I sent Ray a card at Easter and one at Christmas and he sent me one back in return. I also wrote to June Steelwell and she wrote back on many occasions.

The next time we went hopping I had begun working. I worked on a farm in Hersham with my cousin, Carrie. I was so glad that I no longer had to return to school as I hated every moment of it. Schooldays are supposed to be the best and happiest days of your life and for many they were, but not for me. No more nasty children to call me names and laugh at me. I felt happy and free at last.

This year I had packed a lot more clothes than I had ever done before. I had been able to buy myself quite a lot of new things to wear. I would only be wearing jeans during the daytime as I wanted to dress up after tea and go out. I was also very conscious of my speech. I tried hard not to use slang words when I spoke. Carrie laughed at me. "Who do you think yer are, putting on airs and graces. Yer can't make yerself what yer not, ya know. Ya can't get away from what and who yer are."

I knew that, but it wouldn't hurt to try and make something of myself. I was able to wear make-up now without having to wash it off, although my father had a grave dislike for it. Charlie was to stay at home again this year just like last year, as he had a girlfriend called Yvonne.

He was going to bring her down to show her the huts at the farm at the weekend.

Uncle Sammy came and picked us up and off we went, just as we had done year after year, except on the way there was no stopping for a drink, as Sammy was tea total. Uncle Sam didn't believe in smoking or drinking. It was a waste of good money to his mind. "Them fags will kill yer if yer don't stop smoking them," he said to my father, but Dad just laughed. He was always telling my brother, Charlie, not to smoke or drink. "You save yer money and spend it on more important things than sending it up in smoke," he would say.

A STINKING DISCOVERY

As Uncle Sam pulled up in front of the cookhouse, I saw to my dismay that the old stone hut in front of it had gone, and in its place stood a large tin barn. It stretched from the stable right across to the cookhouse. "Oh no," said Mum.

"What's that been put there fer?" I asked.

"How the hell should I know, I don't know," said Mum. "I don't see how we will be able to unpack in the yard; we can't get anywhere near it."

"Oh, stop moaning, woman," said Dad. "We can stop ere and carry the boxes and trunks to the hut."

Uncle Sammy laughed. "Oh lord, you gotta be mad, that's all I can say. I wouldn't come to this place to live like this fer all the tea in China."

Dad glared at him. "Fer Christ's sake, Sam, don't set Mima off. She's bad enough without ya putting your two-penny worth in. You know what she's like."

Sammy laughed all the more. Coral and Barry ran off and the dog went with them. It was just Mum and I left to get the hut straight as Dad had gone to see who was there and who wasn't. "That's it, sod off, Ayres," said Mum. "Leave me to do all the work."

Dad laughed. "What work, yer can make a bed up without me, woman, surely," he said.

I went to the tap and filled the kettle. I could see the Steelwells at the black chicken hut. Uncle Albert wasn't coming this year as my Aunt Liza was very ill with bronchial pneumonia. He was going to come down for a few days, just to see the pickers, if Aunt Liza was well enough.

Aunt Ivy was fussing about putting her things away and shouting at the children as usual. As I walked to our hut, I saw that the yard was piled high with fresh cow dung and, boy, did it stink. Mum was stood with her hands on her hips staring at it. "Oh no, look at that," I said. "What are we going to do? We can't get in the barn with all that lot stuck there, can we."

"Sod the barn," she said. "What about them flies?" "We'll know it when the sun hits that lot, it's right outside our hut. Just look at them flies, Charlie," she shouted. "Come on, look at this. I'm not stopping ere with all this cowshit, it'll give us all a fever."

Dad came marching towards her. "Now what's wrong, Mima?" he said.

"What's wrong? Just cast yer eyes over that lot."

Dad turned to see what Mum was on about. "Oh, my lord," he said. "Whatever possessed them to put that there?" he went on. "I don't know, I just don't know what this place is coming to lately, first the old horses went and now this. I tell yer, I don't know what's happening to this farm, and fancy putting that eyesore in front of the cookhouse." He walked away, shaking his head, mumbling.

"Yer better see Tom about all this dung," shouted Mum. "I'm telling yer now, Charlie, I'm going straight back home with Sammy if yer don't."

Dad said he would go and find Tom and see if it couldn't be shifted. I felt sorry for my father as he hated any sort of change at the farm. You would have thought it belonged to him to hear him talk at times. I think it was the fact we came here year in and year out that made him feel this way and besides, he must have had memories like mine as he had been coming here since he was a child.

Uncle Horace stood swaying to and fro; he couldn't have given a damn what went on as long as the pubs were there.

Mum was still mumbling. "I wonder if the new man would like all this stuck under his nose day and night."

There was a movement on the top of a pile of hay in the new tin barn. Dad had returned and he saw it as well. "Hello," he said, "what's that?" Ray Durman appeared as if out of nowhere. Dad laughed. "Hello, my boy," he shouted. "Don't tell me they bin and got you working fer em now as well." Ray blushed. "Look at im, Horace," said Dad. "He looks like a string bean, don't he."

Ray jumped down and getting on his tractor, he drove off. I called out to him and waved but he took no notice of me. I felt hurt at his attitude towards me as I had so looked forward to seeing him once more. I had thought of him many times during the year and had built up a mental picture of how we would meet. It certainly was not like this. "Ray's in the barn," said Mum. "Did yer see im?"

"Yes," I replied. "I saw him, but he never waved."

"Well, he always was a shy boy," she said. "He'll be around in a few days, you'll see."

After Uncle Sammy had gone home, we sat drinking tea. Dad laughed. "Mima, you must ave brought half the house with us this year. Look at this hut, yer can hardly move."

"Oh, don't be daft," she said. "We got to have somethin to sit on. We don't ave ta live like pigs just because we live in a place like this." I don't know what it was but I had an uneasy feeling as I looked around our little hut. Nothing had changed in it but I felt different somehow.

Aunt Ivy came to the door. "Look, Mima, I got the hopping card so Horace won't be able to sub off it this year and spend all me money, will he?" She ambled off happily.

"Poor old cow!" said Mum. "He spends all her money on drink. It's not fair, ya know, she does work hard."

Mr Durman came to the hut door to speak to Mum and Dad. "Make sure the children keep outta the barn," said Tom. "The new man's given me strict instructions, no children are to go in there."

"Why?" I asked.

"Just do as yer told," said Dad.

Tom smiled. "It's not safe, the tiles are falling through the roof and it's got in a real bad state. You just stay outta it or governor won't be held responsible fer anyone that goes in it."

Mum assured him that we would keep out. A fat chance you got, I thought. I'm going in it no matter what the governor says.

"I see yer got the boy working on the farm with yer, Tom," said Dad. "He's a proper bean pole, ain't he."

Tom laughed. "Yes, he's gotta work now. He won't have time to come up the huts this year, he's to get his rest at night and get stuck into his job." Looking around our hut he said, "You got more in the little hut, Charlie, then I got in my cottage. How the hell did ya fit it all in?"

"It's not me," said Dad. "It's Mima, you ask her."

Tom shook his head as he walked off laughing.

LOUIE'S BOYFRIEND

Louie now had a boyfriend. His name was Cyril Bone. How we all laughed at her. "You'll be Mrs Bone Louie one day," they said. Louie took it all in her stride as she was used to them laughing at her. Squirrel, they called him and he answered to that name whenever we used it. I think he lived on a pig farm just outside the village but I can't be sure. He would call for Louie and off they would go together, much too every one's amusement.

Vera hadn't come this year as she had started work and found herself a boyfriend back home. I did miss her, as we had spent such a lot of time together. Louie kept on asking me to go out up the pub with her and Cyril as she knew I hadn't got anyone now Vera was not here. "Come on," said Louie. "Come with us, you might meet a boy to go around with. Don't sit around the huts all by yerself. They're all kids and ya can't sit around with a load of kids."

That night, I went to the pub with her and I met a boy from one of the council houses. His name was Johnny Collins. Ray no longer came to the huts to see us, so I started to go around with Johnny, although I did miss Ray. It just did not seem the same without his happy face poking around the hut door at night after work. "I do miss my little Ray of sunshine," said Mum. "It's not the same without him." She so resented my going out with Johnny as she still liked Ray.

I just could not understand why Ray kept away so long as he had come and talked to us every year that we were there. I thought perhaps he had grown out of us. Perhaps he had become like Peter and didn't want to know us. I did feel very hurt by it as I was so fond of him. Johnny Collins was in the army and he wrote to me each day when he went back from leave. Albert's words were to ring in my ears when Tom Durman brought the mail around to us pickers. "One day a boy will send you love letters," and now what cousin Albert had said had come true. I was getting letters from Johnny. I know my mother would have given anything if they had been from Ray. She missed him more than anyone else, I think. "Where is my little Ray of sunshine?" she asked Tom as he handed me my letter. "I don't see him much these days."

"He's too busy," said Tom. "He's got work to do, missus. He ain't got the time to come to the huts. He's got responsibilities now he's at work."

I would often see Ray on his motorcycle with one of the boys from the village, but he never said anything to me. I wondered what I had done to make him so distant and off-hand towards me. My Uncle Horace wasn't much help with matters as he took the greatest pleasure in taunting Ray whenever possible. "You'd better watch out, Ray, my boy," he said. "Yer bin an lost yer sweetheart to a soldier, you better win her back or he'll run off with her." Ray ignored him and walked away blushing, as he blushed something dreadful when the men teased him.

After Johnny went back from his leave, Ray came to the huts with Dennis and Barry and he sat in the cookhouse just like old times, talking and laughing with all the rest of us. I tried to talk to him but he barely answered me as he was so shy. I felt that he wanted to say so much more but just could not bring himself to do so.

YVONNE

Charlie came down for the weekend and he brought his girlfriend, Yvonne, with him to show her the huts. My cousin, Vera, was with them as she also brought her boyfriend to show him around. They arrived by train and took the shortcut across the fields. They had caught the train to Bentley station. I think that Yvonne felt like mangling Charlie as she was wearing her best shoes at the time.

My Uncle Albert was down and he was sitting in the cookhouse when they finally got there. I shall never forget his face when he first set eyes on Yvonne. "Blimey, boy, she's a big-un," he said, as he looked Yvonne up and down like some prize heifer. If looks could kill, I think he would have dropped dead on the spot. Yvonne was that mad at his rudeness towards her. The rest of the pickers laughed at her discomfort to make matters worse. I don't think she had ever met a person like my uncle before and, of course, she was a Gorgia (non gypsy folk). She wasn't one of us. Vera's boyfriend was a skinny little thing in comparison to her and Uncle Albert made fun of them just as much.

As the children of the travellers were growing up, they seemed to be breaking away from traditional ways. None of them were marrying their own kind. Very soon the gypsy blood would be no more as it was gradually being depleted.

Yvonne was not at all impressed with what she saw, if fact I think it was quite a shock. Unless you were used to living rough and making do, hop picking was not the sort of holiday that most people would choose, and I could see at a glance that Yvonne was not happy, not one little bit. "That's put her off, Charlie," said Uncle Horace, laughing. "Off fer life, I'd say."

Dad laughed. "She'll just ave ter get used to it if she is to marry into the family," he replied. "She'll ave ter rough it like all the rest of us."

I had my own hop card this year as I was working, I wasn't all that bothered about picking as I felt it didn't matter how much I got. I often went into the woods with Louie and sat on the old tree that had all our family names carved on it. We would sit talking for ages. More often than not my uncle would find us sitting there and he would shout at us and tell us to get back to the bin and pick. What a cheek, I thought, it's my money and I don't have to pick if I don't want to. Louie and I talked about things that had gone on in the past. We still spoke of little Penny from the White Hart. We would reminisce on the old days until it made us close to tears at times. I loved to sit in the woods listening to all the little sounds that you could hear if you only listened with your heart. I felt as though I was trying to store as many of them as I could.

"Listen, Louie," I said. "Can you hear it?"

"Hear what?" she asked. To Louie everything was either black or white. There was no in between. Every now and then a feeling of insecurity would creep over me and fill me with a sense of foreboding. I could not shake it off. I think it was that the farm now had a new owner and there was the constant fear that he was going to get a machine. I found myself taking stock of all the things that surrounded me, no matter how small. It made me more aware of my surroundings, something I had always taken for granted before.

CAUGHT IN THE BARN

After tea on Sunday, I managed to slip into the barn unseen. I knew I would be in trouble if Mum saw me. She kept telling me not to go in there. I lay back in the hay, reading my book, feeling quite content. Mum was up to her armpits in soapy water, doing her washing in a little tin bath in front of the hut. I could see her rubbing the clothes up and down on the scrubbing board. She had a mania for white washing; it had to be spotless. I felt rather smug as I could see her but she couldn't see me. I don't know how long I sat there but I became aware that I was not alone. Looking up, I saw a stranger.

"What are you doing in the barn?" he asked. "I left strict instructions that no one was to come in here."

Oh no, I thought, it must be the new owner of the farm. I didn't know what he looked like as I hadn't seen him before now. My heart sank. I could now see my mother; she was making frantic gestures behind the owner's back to me. She looked like a demented chicken, flapping her arms about in an effort to get me to come out.

"I wasn't doing anything wrong," I said. "I was just reading, that's all."

The man smiled. "What are you reading?" he asked

"Just a book," I replied. "I was just having a read and I didn't touch the hay."

He laughed. "It's not the hay that worries me," he said, "it's the rafters. They're as rotten as can be, and the tiles keep falling through the roof. I should hate to see anyone get hurt through a falling tile. I'm all for young people furthering their education. What's the book about?"

Oh, what a fool I felt, I could hardly tell him it was a love book. I blushed. "It's just a book," I replied, feeling rather silly.

Mum found her voice at last. "Get out of that barn," she yelled. "You know yer ain't supposed ta go in there. I am sorry," Mum said as she walked towards the owner, wiping her hands on her apron as she spoke.

"Tom did tell us pickers not to let the children in the barn and I did tell them, I keep telling them."

The man spoke with a bemused smile on his face, "That's all right, as long as she stays where she is it won't matter. I just don't want her climbing on the beams, that's all. Continue your book," he said, as he turned on his heel and walked away.

Mum went crackers as soon as he was out of sight. "You had ta come in this barn, didn't yer," she said. "It had ta be you that was caught in it, old lady. Well now perhaps you'll take notice the next time yer told somthin. Didn't yer see me trying to tell yer the mush was coming? Didn't yer hear me? No, you had yer head stuck in that book, that's why yer never heard me." She took a swipe at me as I dodged past her. Yes, I thought to myself, trust me to get caught. I still sneaked in there, though, whenever I got the chance to as it was the only place I could read my letters in peace. It was the only place I could think.

BARRY AND DAD

Out in the hop garden during the day, Coral picked hops in her little one-bushel bin that my father had brought her. The dog was sat at her feet dozing in the sun. I was still expected to pick, even though I now worked. Mum made sure of that. Dad came down the hop row towards us. He rolled up a picked bine and sat on it. Mum spread out a cloth and started to get the dinner out. The fire was still smouldering and Dad poked in the ashes for a lighted ember for his cigarette. "Where's Barry?" he asked. "Has he bin back fer his grub?"

My mother gave a deep sigh. "Oh, don't start, Charlie, she said. "He won't pick, so don't go on."

"Go on, go on," my father shouted. "The boy won't pick one hop and you say don't go on. If you didn't pamper the boy all the time and feed him, perhaps,he would do a bit more."

Just then Barry came whistling down the rows towards us, his hands thrust deep in his pockets. "Here he is," said Dad. "He's the little bleeder that won't pick a hop but knows where we are when he wants Tommy." [Tommy meaning food.]

"Oh, shut up, Charlie," Mum moaned. "Leave the boy alone."

"Leave im, leave im," he shouted. "If I give im a few more good hidings he might do a bit more, he might pick like the others."

Barry ducked behind my mother, pulling her apron around his legs in an effort to protect them from Dad's trilby hat. Dad swiped out at him with it but Mum used her body to shield Barry from it. Barry gave me a sneaky grin. My father saw him. He had such big dimples when he smiled and his dark eyes flashed. "I'll make yer laugh, my son," he said. "Just you wait till I get me hands on yer, my boy. You'll be sorry, you'll see if yer ain't. Don't give im no grub, Mima. If he can't pick, he don't eat."

"Oh, don't be daft," said Mum. "The child's gotta eat."

"When he picks, he can eat," said Dad.

Barry darted out from behind Mum. "I don't want any dinner," he said, "so you can stick yer grub."

Dad lunged at him, his face white with anger. I'll make yer talk to me like that, my boy, you'll see if I don't," he said.

Barry fled with a lump of bread and jam in one hand and a jam tart in the other, that Mum had thrust at him. The pickers in the next row laughed and laughed at the sight of my father giving chase as he ran through the rows in pursuit of my brother. Barry stopped when he was a safe distance from my Dad and shouted, "I shan't pick, old man, and yer won't make me." Dad threw his trilby hat at him and Barry stamped all over it, laughing for all he was worth. That's it, I thought, it's the last straw. Dad's hat was his pride and joy. Barry's for it now, and as if that wasn't bad enough, Barry then dived head first into the pokes that were left in the road way for the measurers to collect.

Dad returned out of breath and very angry. "I don't know what to do about that boy," he said. "You've ruined im, Mima. I can't do a thing with him and it's all your fault." He stood trying to catch his breath before trying to speak once more."

"My fault," shouted Mum.

"Yes," said Dad. "You're the one that keeps pampering the boy till I can't do a thing with im." Mum could hardly stop herself from laughing. She had to turn away from Dad so he couldn't see her face. "I can't make it out," said Dad. "My other children have never spoken back at me like he does."

"They picked hops and never so much as looked at me the wrong way let alone answer me back. Even my little girl there picks all day. My Charlie and Sheila were never like im. I blame this on you woman," he said. "This is what becomes of spoiling the boy all the time." He sat down. This is going to be just the same as all the other years, I thought. Barry's not going to pick, no matter how much Dad threatens him, and Mum's still going to take his part, right or wrong. In her eyes he could do no wrong.

Barry still went to the Steelwell's hut a night until they sent him back at bedtime. Mrs Steelwell spoilt Dennis as much as Mum spoilt Barry. They often sat talking and laughing about the antics the two boys got up to.

The week seemed to pass very quickly but they no longer seemed to be the same as they used to. I think it was that the carefree days of my childhood had passed and that I was seeing things in a new light. As I lay in my bed at night, I thought of all the happy times I had spent over the years and I still thought of little Penny from the White Hart. Somehow, I was never able to forget her for very long. I had vivid dreams about her and woke in a cold sweat sometimes.

I lay listening to the sound of the rain as it pitter-pattered on the roof of the hut. I heard my Uncle Horace as he came stumbling up the dip at the side of the huts, singing the one and only song that he knew, *I'll build a castle*. I listened as he tried each hut door in turn until he found the right one. Then I heard my aunt shout as he stumbled into their hut and then it all went quite once more. He never ever got to finish the song as she was always waiting for him with the frying pan ready to knock him out. As I lay watching the flickering shadows on the hut wall, I was aware of the gentle swish of the elderberry branch that swept to and fro across the roof. The past seemed to flash before me like some old movie, especially my younger days. I don't know why but I remembered things more clearly that had taken place when I was small, rather than when I was older somehow. I could picture Dennis Steelwell with his pig, and the dog that fell into the tar well, and countless other things. There had been the time we all went to a wedding in the village church. What a year that was. I don't think that the village had ever had such a wedding like it before.

TANKA'S WEDDING

Tanka was a travelling man who came hop picking. He usually went to Longman's as a rule but this year he came to our farm instead. He had his eye on a widow who had made a camp on the patch of rough grass at the side of our huts by the dip. She had a barrel wagon, a real old gypsy one. It stood on the patch of rough grass with its brasses gleaming and its brightly painted patterns glinting in the sunlight.

Tanka had taken a real shine to the widow and got rather drunk in the Kings Arm's one night and bragged that he was going to ask her to marry him.

The men all bet him that he wouldn't have the nerve to ask her. Well, he did so the laugh was on them. They were married in the church in the village and after we all went into the Kings Arm's, well, the grown-ups did. We stayed outside. I shall never forget that day. The little church was bursting at the seams. I don't think it had ever had so many people in it as it did that day. When the pubs closed, my aunts and uncles all went into the fields opposite the church and they danced and sang whilst their daughters gave out the food that my aunts had taken to eat. Uncle Jim Lane began to play the spoons up and down his legs as my other uncle called the tune for my aunts to dance to. Aunt Carrie and Aunt Louie linked arms and danced around, their plaid skirts swirling around their ankles. They dressed as if time had stood still. They wore black lace up boots with their long skirts and white blouses with a shawl around their shoulders. They wore gold buckle rings on their fingers and gold hoop earrings. They also had gold cameo broaches at the neck of their blouses.

My Uncle Jim Brazil put down a plank of wood for the men to tap dance on as the rest of us looked on, clapping in time to the tune. They danced and sang until it was dark, then we went home to the huts to finish it off in the cookhouse. My cousin, Mushy Lane, was nursing a badly bruised hand. He had got it from winning a bet. There had been a man in the King's Arms pub who was betting every one that he could punch a wall and not call out in pain. What Mushy didn't know was the man he was against had no feeling in his right hand, so he was able to punch walls and not feel a thing, but Mushy did. He would never make a daft bet like that again in a hurry, I know.

Yes, I had seen a lot of things over the past few years and I had met a lot of people, all from different walks of life from all over the country.

We met each year in the little village of Binstead for a few short weeks to pick hops. I suppose to people who had never been, we must have looked and sounded rather strange, as we had our own way of talking and of doing things. Hop picking is either in your blood or it isn't; you either loved it or hated the sight of it. I just loved it like my father.

I eventually fell asleep. The next day was to be the last day for another year. We had picked all the hops in Bull Pit and so we would have to pick the remainder in Lipskins. We had to go through the woods to reach it as it was right over the other side of the wood. It was only a little hop garden. We just picked a few from it each year so as to make up the quota for the farm. We left the rest. The picker's trekked through the woods with their baskets on their backs in a long line as it was the quickest way to reach it. We could walk to it if we went down the road and turned left to the cart track, it was just past the post office. This was the way we reached it after the first day as it was in a different direction than the other hop fields. Mum didn't mind as she was able to get her shopping on the way home now without having to go out of the way to get it.

BINNING

"You had better make sure you got yer jeans on today, Sheila," said Mum as I started to get dressed. "The men and boys will be about, binning the girls if they can. Ya don't want ter get caught out, do yer now, if they bin yer."

"I'm not getting caught, so don't you worry about it," I replied. Binning is done on the last day of picking hops. It's a tradition that's gone on for as long as I can remember.

I quickly dressed and went outside. It looked as though it might be a nice day. It was one of those misty mornings. The morning air had a bite to it and it took my breath away. I could hear my Uncle Horace calling to his children to get up. "Were not finished yet," he said, "so shake a leg and get up." I went into the cookhouse and sat down. The fire was just about alight. My Uncle Horace came in and gave it a kick. He then took a stick from a bavin and poked it, before breaking it up and sticking it in the middle of the fire. It burst into flames, sending sparks spitting all over the place, just like a fireworks cracker. "Stand back," he said, "if yer don't want to get burnt keep back." I jumped back, my eyes stinging from the smoke and my throat burning as I gasped for breath.

As I turned away from the fire, I could see the mist over the far side of the field. It was still lingering under the hedgerows by the orchard fence. As I stood deep in thought, my father shouted at me to get going. "Come on, Sheila, stop day dreaming, we got work ter do. We ain't finished just yet, yer know. There ain't nothin in that field that yer ain't seen before."

All day long I felt uneasy as I could see the older boys creeping about on the lookout for some unsuspecting girl to bin. Louie came screaming towards us but the boys caught up with her and shoved her head first into Mum's bin. They stood back laughing. "Oh no, Louie," said Mum, as she helped her out of her hop picking basket. "You always get caught, don't yer Louie." I could see that my mother was finding it very hard not to laugh at Louie.

Louie began to scream at the top of her voice. "You just wait till I tell me father about this you lot, you'll cop it when he finds out, just see if yer don't." The boys laughed at her all the more.

What a sight she was. She had hops in her hair and up her nose; they even stuck to her clothing. She shook from head to toe. I felt so sorry for her. Suddenly the boys turned their attention on me. I quickly sat down. "I think that it's about time you got binned, Sheila," said my cousin, Henry Ayres. "You ain't had a taste of the hops, ave yer."

"No and I don't want ter," I shouted. "So keep yer distance or else Ill set the dog on yer." I grabbed at our dog; he was snapping and snarling at them. Shane was not a nasty dog but he sensed that I was in danger and he was very protective of me. It was all I could do to hold him back.

"We can wait," said Henry. "Ya wont ave that dog all the time to protect yer."

My sister had been hiding behind Mum whist all the commotion was going on. She was scared stiff. "They won't do that to me, will they?" she asked in a nervous voice. "They won't stick me head first in a basket will they?"

"No," said Mum, "they only do it to big girls like Louie, not little girls like you."

Coral looked relived. "They going to do it to Sheila then?" she asked.

"No," I shouted, "they ain't."

Mum just smiled and said, "We'll see."

Louie was still shaking, in a state of shock. "They didn't see me drawers, did they?" she asked.

"No, Louie," I said. "No, yer dress never went up that high, they didn't see a thing." I tied the dog to my basket to make sure that the boys didn't get to me. I was not about to take any chances with them.

The whistle went for dinner and we stopped work. Dad had returned and was busy rolling up a picked bine to sit on. "Well," he said, "about another hour or so and that will be that fer this year I reckon."

"Do yer think so?" said Mum. "There's still a lot of hops left."

Dad sat back. Taking off his trilby hat, he fanned his face with it. It was funny how hot it got about lunch time as the mornings were so cold to start with. I was suddenly aware of wood pigeons cooing to each other, and the sound of buzzing bees as they went about their work collecting pollen from the wild flowers in the hedgerows. The gifts of nature that we all take for granted. "Listen to that, Mima," said Dad, as he leaned back on one elbow. "Yer won't hear that in Moseley Close, will yer."

Mum tilted her head to one side; she had to agree with him. Although she would never admit it, she had come to terms with going hop picking. I think that now we were all older she had more time to enjoy herself, and when she moaned it was out of habit, nothing more. I could hear the murmuring voices of the other pickers as they sat eating and talking.

"I won't be long," I called as I made my way through the rows to meet Louie. I still kept a sharp lookout for the boys as I knew that they wouldn't let up on me till I had been binned. Louie and I went into the wood with the dog scampering at our side.

"Me dad said that we won't be coming no more," said Louie. "He reckons that we won't pick no more hops after today."

"Oh, don't be silly, Louie," I replied. "Of course we will."

The sunlight sifted through the branches of the trees in silver streams of light and the air was cool. We sat on a log that had all our family names carved on it and I could not help but notice the red and white mushrooms that grew by its side. I gently touched them with the tip of my boot. "Don't do that," said Louie. "Them red ones is poisonous, me dad said so."

264

"I know, I know," I replied. "He told us often enough, didn't he."

She shrugged. "Where's the dog? I can't see him." I had forgotten all about him until now. He must have run off while we were talking. We looked about us frantically; we knew we were in a fix if the boys should find us. I called the dog; there was no reply, no bark and no scamper of leaves that could be him. I shouted once more, "Listen," said Louie. She put a finger to her mouth "I can hear boys," she said. "I can hear something." I could hear it now and it was the boys. We slipped quietly from the wood, only stopping to take shelter behind some bushes when the boys passed us close by.

"Phew, that was close," we both said.

"I thought we had it that time," said Louie.

I felt rather sad as we walked from the wood. Louie's words kept ringing in my ears, me dad said we won't be picking again is what she said. "Do yer really think the new man will get a machine, Louie?" I asked.

"Well, me dad reckons he will," she said. "All the other farms hereabout's ave got em, ain't they." I looked all around me at the trees and plants, how pretty they all looked. It was so peaceful.

When we got back to the hop garden we picked for an hour or so and then the whistle went. "All off," shouted Tom Durman.

"That's it for another year," said Dad "No more hops to pick." I thought I detected sadness in his voice.

"Good job too," said Mum as she picked up our few belongings. Dad gave a deep sigh as he looked at her. His face was as long as a fiddle. We made our way home to the huts and I looked about me at the surrounding countryside. I suppose I got my love of the country from my father. As we passed the tar well, I thought about the dog that had fallen into it. I again felt that I must take stock of my surroundings. I felt in my heart that it would be the last time I should see them. Tired and weary, we crossed the road by the forge and climbed the steep bank at the side of the huts. The only thing left to be done was pay out day.

I sat in the cookhouse with my friends and other pickers that night until quite late, all of us laughing and joking as we had done on countless other occasions, but there were long silences in between the laughter. We all knew it was to be the last night for us all. We didn't need telling. We joked about seeing each other again, but we knew it would not be so. Reluctantly, I said my good nights and went to bed but it would be a long time till sleep claimed me that night.

PAYING OUT DAY

The next day we got up rather later than we usually did. It was paying out day at the farm. I helped Mum pack and then went with her and Dad to the Golding's Cottage. That was where we had to go to get paid. I felt rather nervous, as I had never been before. A crowd of pickers walked just ahead of us as we crossed the potato field. We slid down the steep bank in front of the Goldings' cottage and joined the pickers that were there. Just outside the Durman's cottage was along table. The owner was sitting at it with some of the men that worked on the farm.

The owner had Tom's ledger in front of him. I think that the men were there just in case of any trouble. Tom called out to the pickers by name in alphabetical order. We then went in turn to the table to get paid. As we were Ayres, we were first. Mum and Dad went up, then me. I walked to the table when Tom called my name and he handed me a packet with money in it and said, "Don't spend it all at once, Sheila, put some in the bank." I thanked him and then joined Mum and Dad. We had to wait for my Uncle Horace and Aunt Ivy to get paid as we had to walk back to the huts with them. Some of the pickers could get rather nasty if they thought they had not got the amount of money that they thought they had coming. That was the reason the farm hands were about. My uncle was the one; he would sub so much during picking that there was hardly anything left to come on pay day. This year, my Aunt Ivy had kept hold of her hop picking card so that my uncle could not get a sub from it.

"Oh, look at that," said Mum. "She is so happy, it's the first year that she's got all her hopping money."

"She won't be fer long when she has to give it all to Horace," said Dad.

"Why?" asked Mum. "What has she got to give it to I'm fer?"

"Well, he's been getting drunk on the slate from the new man at the White Hart, and he's gotta pay the man," said Dad. "He's gotta go past the pub to go home, so he can't not pay the man, can he now."

"Oh, my poor Ivy," said Mum. "It's not fair, he drinks all her money away."

"Come on, Sheila," said Dad. "Put that money away in yer pocket, yer never know who's about on pay day."

As soon as we reached the huts, I came down to earth with a bang. "Give yer mum the money, Sheila," said Dad.

"No," I said, "it's mine, I earned it didn't I? Tom gave it to me for the hops that I picked. It's mine."

"Give it to yer mother like I told yer", he said. "Yer have ta pay yer way in this life, yer ave ta give it to yer mother, girl. Give yer mother the money or you'll feel the back of me hand."

I handed her the packet.

"I'll buy you a coat form C&A," she said as she took it. She promised I could choose one when we got back. I knew it was useless to argue with them about it so I had to give in. Besides, she would not let Johnny Collins stay at our house if I didn't. Johnny was going to come and see me when I got back home to Hersham. He was going to get a weekend pass so that he could come to see me. He would have to stay with us at our home or he would not get back in time if he didn't.

"I'm never going to go hop picking ever again," I said to Mum. "I'm not going to pick fer nothin."

"Oh yes yer will," said Mum. "When it comes to going ter Hampshire, yer as bad as yer father, and if yer think that he will let yer stay behind like Charlie, well yer can think again, cos he won't."

I went out with Johnny for a few weeks but it fizzled out. I didn't really want him; he was just a bit of fun as Ray had not been about for me to go out with. That's the only reason why I went out with Johnny in the first place, and my mother knew it. "I wish you had a boyfriend like Ray," she said. "He was such a lovely boy. I don't know what happened to him. Why couldn't you have landed up with him?" I wish I knew the reason myself but I didn't, so that was that.

THE MACHINES TAKE OVER

Well, that was the last time that we were to go hop picking, as a letter came sometime later in the year to tell us that our services were no longer required. It asked us to collect our belongings from our hut if we wanted them. The farm had now replaced us with a hop picking machine, so we were not needed. My father was heartbroken when he read the letter. He looked so sad. "I told yer he would get a machine, Charlie," said Mum. "I just knew he would, no matter what he promised Mr Paul when he brought the farm from him."

"Mr Paul said he wouldn't," said my dad. "That's the reason he sold it to him. He said he would keep us pickers on. He said he was not getting a bloody machine." Dad threw the letter down in disgust. I picked it up and read the last few lines that asked us to collect our belongings. "Well if he thinks I'm going all that way just fer a brass bed, he can think again, cos I'm not," said Dad. I felt numb. How could they do this to us? We always went hop picking. It was our holiday. It was the only one we could afford. My father gave a deep sigh. "Well, I tell yer now," he said, "it will never pick like us. It can never pick like the human hand can. I've been going to that farm man and boy, I ave." Sadly, he walked away. He had been going to that very farm since he was a young boy. He knew every stick and stone on the place. He had only missed one year and that was the year I was born.

My mind flashed back to the hop fields after a hard day's work and the journey back to the huts. I could see it all so clearly now in my mind. I felt glad that I had taken stock of my surroundings on that last day. There would be no more walks in the woods on hot sunny days to get fresh water from the spring. I would no longer be able to sit in the old barn as I had done so many times in the past. It was the end of an era an end to a way of life that I had loved and known all my lifetime until now.

It was the end for my father, too, as he had been going since he was a baby in his mother's arms, and it cut him to the quick. Now when I see him fondle the wild hops that grow in the fields where we live, I see a faraway look in his eyes and I know he is thinking of those bygone days of long long ago, when we all went away on our holidays.

Well, September has just been and gone and what I would not give if just once more I could hear my father say, "Come on, Shill, ain't yer ready, were going hopping today."

The end

END NOTE

The year is 1983 and I am forty-two years old. I felt a compelling urge to write down all my wonderful memories of my hop picking holidays. Hop picking is now a thing of the past. I have often told my own children about the things we did when we went on our hopping holiday. I know they find it hard to believe that we lived in such poor conditions at the farm when we went. I have since been back to Binstead; yes, it's still there, although it has changed over the years.

My husband, Norman, and I have stayed at the Cedars pub. The square of rough grass has gone and in its place is a car park. The little shop at its side is now a lounge bar where food is served. The chapel is no longer there as it is part of the car park at the Cedars pub. The White Hart is now a private house and the stone wall by its side is all covered in shrubs. At its side stands a modern house surrounded by conifers, completely out of keeping with its surroundings and the character of the place. People in the village have changed over the years as outsiders buy up the empty houses for country retreats as and when they become empty. The up and coming youngsters cannot afford to buy them and so they leave the village to look for pastures new. The roads have been widened and the hedgerows cut. Almost all the old ways are going and farms are not as they used to be.

When I was small, horses and carts were used on the farm. The work was done by men and not machines. The farmers kept cattle and all sorts of livestock, but now corn is growing in their place. The hop picking machine that replaced us pickers has gone, owing to the cheap hops from abroad and the introduction of chemical beers. It has put an end to hop farming on most British farms. The hop gardens are now bare, the poles and wires all gone at Hay Place Farm. The woods I once played in are all gone, as well as the hedgerows. They were taken away so that the fields could be made bigger to have a more profitable harvest. The hop kiln has been taken down and the farm rebuilt.

The Goldings' cottage where the Durmans live is still there and they make tea for my parents whenever they call to see them. They talk about old times at the farm with Tom and Ivy Durman. The huts are still standing, although in a state of decay. The old stone barn has gone and the stables as well. Even the tin barn that was put up the last year that we came was gone. In their place stands a big tin barn the size of an aircraft hangar; it covers the yard right up to the huts. It even covers part of the cookhouse as well. The huts were used as cowsheds in the end. That was what my mother had said they looked like and were good for all those years ago. I felt sad as I stood in the cookhouse, our ashes still in the fireplace. I looked out at the field, now full of corn. I could picture it as it was all those years ago, with children playing tag on starry nights. I could almost hear the murmuring voices of hoppers of long ago and smell the smoke from the cooking fires.

I ask myself what will be left of the place in a few more years. Not much, I think. I worry about the future of all farms as we cannot expect the land to go on producing corn year after year, when it's not needed. Why grow mountains of unwanted corn I feel our generation will pay the price, if not the next. I wonder what our children will have. Will it be memories like ours? I think not, as I had a way of life that was hard but, oh, so rewarding in a way not easily understood at times. I would not change a moment of it. I have learned things that a school could never teach you, things that people could never know unless they lived it.

I have heard Binstead church had a very distinguished guest in it. Lord Montgomery was laid to rest in its church yard when he passed away. My husband and I found his resting place when we went to the church and signed the visitors' book.

I also accomplished another thing, and that was finding young Penny Yalden's grave. I felt rather strange standing by her grave as here was I, a grandmother, keeping my promise to her after all these years. I returned with my daughter, Penny, and we placed flowers on her grave together. Yes, my daughter is named after her, as I was unable to forget the little girl that I had befriended from the White Hart. I had promised to find her one day and I had. I gave my first child her name. I may not have a great education, but I have memories much more precious to me than all the Olevels and degrees in the world.

I feel privileged to have been one of the hop pickers' children at Hay Place Farm.

In 1984, Ray Durman contacted me by letter. He and his wife, also named Sheila, met up with my husband and myself. We went to stay with them in Wiltshire. My mother was later to see her little Ray of Sunshine, at her ninetieth birthday party.

This was her ninetieth birthday surprise. She was so overwhelmed, stating he was the best birthday present she had ever had. Ray and I have stayed in contact ever since.

In 2014, Peter Yalden, Penny's twin brother found out where I lived. He and his mother had tried to trace me for years. His mother wanted to thank me for the flowers I left on Penny's grave. This was a large broken heart wreath of cream roses. This was followed by a crinoline doll in flowers the year after, that I had made myself. This said, "From your little hop picker friend from hut one."

Unfortunately, his mother had passed away before she could find me to say thank you for remembering Penny. I now feel that my life has come full circle, and that my bucket list is full. I am overjoyed that Peter took the time to find me sixty years later.